COULTER LIBRARY ONONDAGA COMM. COLL.

3   0418   00225080   9

SEX EDUCATION: AN ISLAMIC PERSPECTIVE

EDITED BY
SHAHID ATHAR

FOREWORD BY
HASSAN HATHOUT

SIDNEY B. COULTER LIBRARY
Onondaga Community College
Syracuse, New York 13215

© Shahid Athar, 1995

All rights reserved. No part of this book may be reproduced or utilized in any form or by any means, electronic or mechanical, including photocopying and recording or by any information storage and retrieval system, without the written permission of the publisher. All inquiries may be sent to the distributor, KAZI Publications, Inc.

Library of Congress Cataloging in Publication Data

Athar, Shahid (editor)
     Sex Education: An Islamic Perspective

     Includes bibliographical references.
     1. Muslims. I. Athar, Shahid (editor) II. Title

ISBN: 0-934905-30-4

Published by
The Library of Islam
P. O. Box 595
South Elgin IL 60177

Distributed by
KAZI Publications, Inc.
3023 W. Belmont Avenue
Chicago IL 60618
Tel: 312-267-7001; FAX: 312-267-7002

In the Name of God, the Merciful, the Compassionate

To Prophet Muhammad,
the mercy to mankind,
our teacher and guide.
May God's mercy and peace be with him
and his family. (Amin)

CONTENTS

PREFACE

Sex in the mind of some parents is a dirty word. They are uncomfortable in discussing it with their teenagers just as their own parents never discussed it with them. They leave it up to the Sunday school to teach Islam and up to the television and the secular school system to teach sex education.

Thanks to the "birds and the bees" who taught mankind that sex is natural and a gift from God. No one can deny the power of sex and the built-in desires. A powerful genie, if not brought into submission to the Will of God, is certainly capable of causing tremendous destruction of the lofty Islamic morals which Islam builds for its believers.

Muslim parents and teenagers are getting mixed messages about their roles. They are torn between what seems to be an Islamic perspective and what is actually being taught by the secular media and the education system. Children develop right and wrong concepts not from the books but from what they see on the television and what they see around them.

For some of today's youngsters, it may not be enough to be told that they should not engage in sex because Islam forbids it. They also need to be advised of the hazards of early sex, sexually transmitted diseases, teenage pregnancy and sex education in the dimension of marriage and sex after marriage, in addition to the biology of development and hormonal changes at puberty. Their frank questions about sex should not be avoided but need honest answers from the Islamic perspective.

In this book I have attempted to address all these issues. I have begun each chapter with a quotation from like-minded American sex educators to emphasize that this concern is common to both Muslims and non-Muslims. I pray for the soul of my mentor, the late Dr. Mahmoud Abu Saud, who played a "grandfather's role" for my own children and many, many Muslim youth. I thank the editors of *Minaret* and the *Journal of the Islamic Medical* Association for allowing me to use the informative articles of Farhad Khan and Dr. Hamad, respectively. I also thank Dr. Ahmed El-Kadi and Dr. Iman El-Kadi for their permission to use the late Dr. Abu Saud's article, "Sex Roles in Muslim Families in the USA." Above all, I thank Muslim youth, including my own children, for asking me most intelligent and sometimes difficult questions. I also thank Dr. Laleh Bakhtiar for reviewing the manuscript and KAZI Publications for publishing it. May God accept the efforts of those who strive in His cause.

Shahid Athar, M.D.
June 1, 1995
Indianapolis, Indiana

FOREWORD

Some time ago I was on an Islamic tour in Canada. My hosts took me to the Islamic center in one city. They proudly told me that the building had been a Christian church until bought by the Muslim community and transformed into a mosque/Islamic center. The architecture of the church revealed the history of the building. It was quite an emotional experience to hear the *adhan* and observe the Islamic prayers in this place. Then my hosts took me to another city. Their faces gleamed joyfully as they introduced me to a second surprise in one day: the mosque had also been a church and then bought by Muslims. Barely containing their jubilance, they asked me, "Describe your feelings, doctor." I answered, "I feel very scared!" It was a shocking response to them until I explained that the pertinent question to ask should be, "What made the Christians sell their churches to Muslims?" A generation of observing Christians was followed by another generation who could care less for religion or the church. The inevitable thought to follow was whether the same could not happen to Muslims. Unless the coming generation grows up to be active, genuine Muslims, the chain will be broken and—God forbid—our current masjids and centers might be on the market for sale in a decade or two.

The challenge facing Muslim parents, centers and mosques is obviously tremendous, given the sad state of licentiousness and moral disintegration pervading Western society. At the top of the list comes the sexual revolution with its vagaries that are too obvious to describe. Not only do our young people have the natural sexual instinct as their bodies beam with hormones, but they are also subjected to a tidal wave of neo-morality providing stimulation, inflammation, promotion, commercialization, easy access, rationalization and brain-washing into new social norms that conflict with Islam and with all divine religions.

How do we prepare our children to confront this temptation and be victorious over it? How do we train soldiers for battle? How do we vaccinate our children to acquire immunity against that to which they will inevitably be exposed?

Many Muslim families and indeed Muslim leaders and preachers have no real answer. Some think that children will remain children and others believe that because we are observant Muslims then our children will—naturally—follow in our steps. To bury our heads in the sand is no good and is a betrayal of our Islamic obligations to our children.

Dr. Shahid Athar is one of the small band of Muslims whose conscience made it incumbent on them to stand up and try to neutralize this gaping deficit. In my knowledge of him, I found a man who is keen on serving Islam with his mind and soul, rather than with rhetoric and sloganism so abundant in our ranks. He is among the few whose vision is more focused on tomorrow rather than the fleeting hustle and bustle of today. Unless the real issues are addressed, the future will be bleak.

In this book, Dr. Athar establishes the diagnosis and prescribes the treatment. I hope it will be read with an open mind by the Muslim youth and especially by their parents, teachers and preachers.

It is indeed my privilege to write this foreword. My God bless my brother Shahid.

Hassan Hathout

1
SEX EDUCATION, TEENAGE PREGNANCY, SEX IN ISLAM AND MARRIAGE

SHAHID ATHAR

❝If you tell kids about sex, they'll do it. If you tell them about VD, they'll go out and get it. Incredible as may seem, most oppositions to sex education in this country are based on the assumption that knowledge is harmful. But research in this area reveals that ignorance and unresolved curiosity, not knowledge, are harmful. Our failure to tell children what they want and need to know is one reason we have the highest rates of out-of-wedlock teens pregnancy and abortion of any highly developed country in the world."

"What Kids Need to Know,"
Psychology Today, October 1986. Dr. Sol Gordon,
Professor Emeritus, Syracuse University,
and an expert on sex education

"Say: Are they equal those who know, and those who do not know?" (39:9). "Blessed are the women of the Helpers. Their modesty did not stand in the way of their seeking knowledge about their religion" (Bukhari and Muslim).

INTRODUCTION

Although the Quran has placed so much emphasis on acquiring knowledge, and in the days of Prophet Muhammad (ﷺ) Muslim men and women were never too shy to ask him questions including those related to private affairs such as sexual life, for Muslim parents of today, sex is a dirty word. They feel uncomfortable in discussing sex education with their children, but do not mind the same being taught at their children's school by secular or non-Muslim teachers (of even the opposite sex), by their peers of either sex, and by the media and television. An average child is exposed to 9000 sexual scenes per year.

These parents should know that sex is not always a dirty word. It is an important aspect of our life. God Who cares for all the aspects of our life, and not just the way of worshiping Him, discusses reproduction, creation, family life, menstruation and even ejaculation in the Quran. Prophet Muhammad (ﷺ), who was sent to us as an example, discussed many aspects of sexual life including sexual positions with his Companions.

The main reason Muslim parents do not or cannot discuss sex education with their children is because of the their cultural upbringing, not their religious training. They are often brought up in a state of ignorance in regard to sex issues. As a result, they may not be comfortable with their own sexuality or its expression. They leave Islamic education to Islamic Sunday schools and sex education to American public schools and the media.

WHAT IS SEX EDUCATION AND WHO SHOULD GIVE IT?

Is sex education about knowing the anatomy and physiology of the human body or about the act of sex or about reproduction and family life or about prevention of sexually transmitted diseases and unwanted pregnancy? Is giving sex ed equivalent to permission in engaging in sex? One

Figure 1: Pregnancy Profile (reprinted with the permission of *Time Magazine*).

Figure 2: An American Dilemma (reprinted with the permission of *Time Magazine*).

PREGNANCY PROFILE
Each figure equals 5 pregnancies

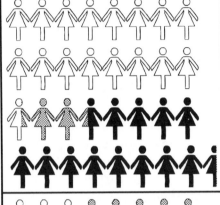

Black Teens
163 per 1,000

51% Nonmarital births

8% Marital births

41% Abortions

White Teens
83 per 1,000

19% Nonmarital births

35% Marital births

47% Abortions

AN AMERICAN DILEMMA
Pregnancy rates per 1,000 teenage females
Each figure equals 10 pregnancies

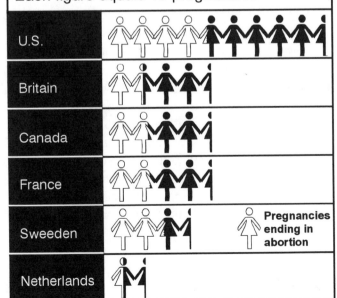

U.S.

Britain

Canada

France

Sweden

Pregnancies ending in abortion

Netherlands

sex educator at my son's school told the parents, "I am not planning to tell your children whether or not they should engage in sex or how to do it but in case they decide to do it, they should know how to prevent sexually transmitted diseases (STD), venereal diseases (VD), acquired immune deficiency syndrome (AIDS) and pregnancy."

The problem with this is that at the present time sex ed as taught in the public schools is incomplete. It does not cover morality associated with sex, sexual dysfunctions and deviations and the institution of marriage.

One of the basic questions is, "Do children need sex education?" Do you teach a baby duck how to swim or just put it in the water and let it swim? After all, for thousands of years men and women have been having sex without any formal education. In many traditional civilizations, sex education starts after marriage and with trial and error. Some couples learn it faster than others and do it better than others due to difference in sexual perception and expression of one partner. In my opinion having a dozen children is not necessarily proof of their love. An appropriate and healthy sex education is crucial to the fulfillment of a happy marriage.

With regard to the question who should teach sex ed, I believe everyone has to play his or her role. Parents have to assume a more responsible role. A father has a duty to be able to answer his son's questions and a mother has the same duty to her daughter. We can hardly influence the sex ed taught in public schools or by the media, but we can supplement that with an ethical and moral dimension adding family love and responsibility. Apart from these players, some role can be played by Sunday school teachers, the family physician, the pediatrician and the clergy. Within a family, the older sister has a duty towards the younger one and the elder brother has a duty towards younger ones.

SEX EDUCATION IN AMERICAN SCHOOLS

Sex education is given in every American school, public or private, from grades 2 to 12. The projected 1990 cost to the nation was $2 billion per year. Teachers are told to give technical aspects of sex ed without telling the students about moral values or how to make the right decisions. After describing the male and female anatomy and reproduction, the main emphasis is on the prevention of venereal diseases and teenage pregnancy. With the rise of AIDS, the focus is on 'Safe Sex' which means

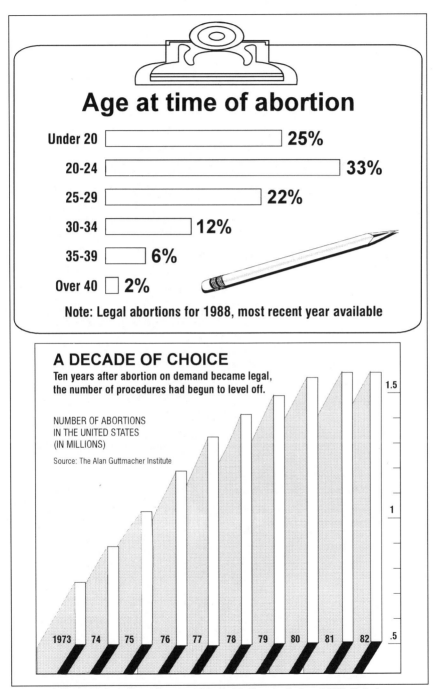

Figure 3: Age at the Time of Abortion (reprinted with the permission of *USA Today*)

Figure 4: A Decade of Choice (reprinted with the permission of *Time Magazine*).

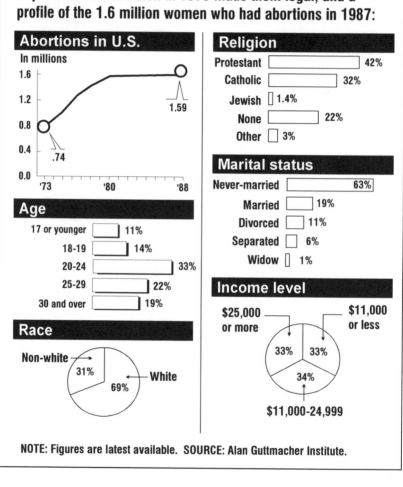

Who has abortions?
Number of abortions performed since Roe vs. Wade Supreme Court decision in 1973 made them legal, and a profile of the 1.6 million women who had abortions in 1987:

Abortions in U.S.
In millions

1.6
1.2
0.8 — .74
0.4
0.0

'73   '80   '88

1.59

Religion
Protestant 42%
Catholic 32%
Jewish 1.4%
None 22%
Other 3%

Marital status
Never-married 63%
Married 19%
Divorced 11%
Separated 6%
Widow 1%

Age
17 or younger 11%
18-19 14%
20-24 33%
25-29 22%
30 and over 19%

Income level
$25,000 or more — $11,000 or less
33%   33%
34%
$11,000-24,999

Race
Non-white 31%
White 69%

NOTE: Figures are latest available. SOURCE: Alan Guttmacher Institute.

Figure 5: Who has abortions? (reprinted with the permission of *Time Magazine*).

having condoms available each time you decide to have sex with someone you don't know. With the help of our tax dollars, about 76 schools in the country have started dispensing free condoms and contraceptives to those who go to school health clinics. Very soon there will be vending machines in school hallways where 'children' can get a condom each time they feel like having sex.

The role of parents is minimized by American sex educators and sometimes ridiculed. In one of the sex ed movies I was made to watch a film called, "Am I Normal?" as a parent at my son's school. Whenever the young boy asks his father a question about sex, the father, shown as a bum and a slob, shuns him and changes the topic. Finally the boy learns it from a stranger and then is shown going into a movie theater with his girlfriend.

Sex education as promoted by some Western educators is devoid of morality is in many ways unacceptable to our value system. The examples of the teachings of one such educator are:

a. Nudity in homes (in shower or bedroom) is a good and healthy way to introduce sexuality to smaller (under 5) children, giving them an opportunity to ask questions. At the same time, in the same book, he also states that 75% of all child molestation and incest (500,000 per year) occur by a close relative (parent, step-parent or another family member).

b. A child's playing with genitals of another child is a permissible 'naive exploration' and not a reason for scolding or punishment. He is also aware that boys as young as 12 have raped girls as young as 8. We don't know when this 'naive exploration' becomes a sex act.

c. Children caught reading dirty magazines should not be made to feel guilty, but parents should use it as a chance to get some useful points across to him or her about sexual attitudes, values and sex exploitation. Like charity, pornography should start at home!

d. If your daughter or son is already sexually active, instead of telling them to stop, the parent's moral duty is to protect their health and career by providing them information and means for contraception and avoiding VD. Maybe this its true for rebellious teens and their submissive parents!

Educators like the one referred to above do not believe that giving sexual information means giving the OK for sex. I just wonder as to why some folks after being told the shape, color, smell and taste of a new fruit, and pleasures derived from eating it, would not like to try it? These educators say that even if your child does not ask any questions about sex,

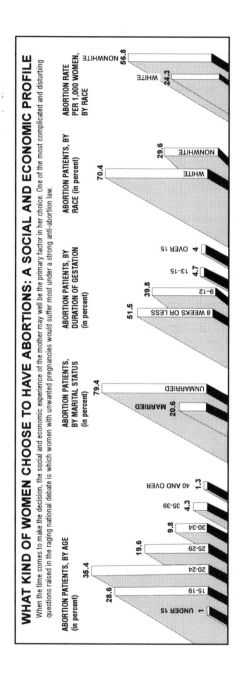

Figure 6: What Kind of Women Choose to Have Abortions (reprinted with the permission of *Newsweek Magazine*).

parents should initiate the discussion using i.e. a neighbors pregnancy, a pet's behavior, advertisement, popular music or a TV show. I wonder why these educators are obsessed with loading children with sexual information whether they want it or not.

THE MORE THEY KNOW IT —THE MORE THEY DO IT

Sex education in American schools has not helped decrease the teenager incidence of VD or teenage pregnancy. This is because it has not changed their sex habits. According to Marion Wright Elderman, President of the Children' Defense Fund, in a recent report, out of every twenty teens, ten are sexually active but only four use conceptions, two get pregnant and one gives birth. In 1982, a John Hopkins study found one out of every five 15 year olds, and one in three 16 year olds are sexually active. The incidence increased to 43% in 17 year olds. The Louis Harris poll in 1986 found that 57% of the nations 17 year olds, 46% of 16 year olds, 29% 15 year old were sexually active. Now it is estimated that about 80% of girls entering college had sexual intercourse at least once. Going to church does not help either. 1438 teenagers, mostly white, attending conservative evangelical church were sent questions about their sex life. 26% of 16 year olds, 35% of 17 year olds, and 43% of 18 year olds said they had sexual intercourse at least once. 33% that responded also said sex outside of marriage was morally acceptable.

HAZARDS OF EARLY SEX

The health hazards of early sex includes sexual trauma, increase in incidence of cervical cancer, sexually transmitted disease and teenage pregnancy. We will take up each individually. A variety of injuries are possible and do happen when sex organs are not ready for sex in terms of full maturation. Some of these injuries have a long lasting effect·· Cervical cancer has been thought to be related to sex at an early age and with multiple partners. Dr. Nelson and his associates in their article on epidemiology of cervical cancer call it a sexually transmitted disease.

TEENAGE PREGNANCY

About one million or more teenage girls become pregnant every year, at a rate of 3000 per day, 80% of whom are unmarried. Out of this 1 million, about 500,000, decide to keep their baby, and 450,000 are aborted (or ? murdered). 100,000 decide to deliver and give the baby up for adoption. In 1950 the incidence of birth from unmarried teenagers was only 13.9%, but in 1985 it increased to 59%. It is a myth that teenage pregnancy is a problem of the black and poor. To the contrary 2/3 teens getting pregnant now are white, suburban and above the poverty income level. The pregnancy rate (without marriage) in 54,000 enlisted Navy women is 40% as compared to 17% in the general population.

What is the life of those who have teenage pregnancy? Only 50% complete high school and more than 50% of them are on welfare. They themselves become child abusers and their children, when grown up, have 82% incidence of teenage pregnancy. 8.6 billion dollars are spent every year for the financial and health care support of teenage mothers.· The sexual revolution of the 60's has affected another dimension of health care. In 1985 alone, 10 million cases of chlamydia, 2 million cases of gonorrhea, 1 million venereal warts, 0.5 million genital herpes and 90,000 syphilis were diagnosed. The plague of AIDS is adding a new twist to our fears. 200,000 cases have been diagnosed in the US alone, out of which 50% have already died. The disease is growing at a rate of one case every 14 minutes and so far there is no effective treatment. Father Bruce Ritter in New York, who operates shelters for runaway children, says the biggest threat to the nation's 1 million runaways is the threat of AIDS now.

WHY DO CHILDREN GET INVOLVED IN SEX?

There are many reasons why children get involved in sex. The most common is peer pressure. Their common response is "since everybody is doing it." One of the reasons is their desire for sexual competence with adults and a way to get ahead. Another common reason is their lack of self-esteem which they want to improve by becoming a father or mother. Sometimes it is due to a lack of other alternatives to divert their sexual energies. It could also be due to a lack of love and appreciation at home. Detachment from home can lead to attachment elsewhere. Sexual pressure on them is everywhere, at school from their peers, from the TV where about 20,000 sexual scenes are broadcasted in advertisement, soap operas, prime time shows and MTV. The hard core rock music nowadays fans the flames of sexual desires. Most parents do not know what kind of music their children are hearing. If they care and listen to rock songs like Eat Me Alive (Judas Priest), Purple Rain (Prince), Losing It (Madonna), The Last American Virgin, Papa Don't Preach, Private Dancer (Tina Turner), Material Girl (Madonna) and Cyndi Lauper's songs, they will know what they are talking about. The songs have pornographic words and sentences which made Kandy Stroud, a former rock fan, begged parents to stop their children from listening to what she calls 'Pornographic Rock'. This shows music does affect our sexual mood. It does so by activating melatonin, the hormone from the pineal gland in the brain which is turned on by darkness and turned off by flashing lights. It is the same gland which has been thought to trigger puberty and affects the reproductive cycle and sex mood.

WHAT IS THE TRUE ROLE OF PARENTS?

American educators are putting the blame for their failures (i.e. teenage pregnancy) on the parents. In fact in Wisconsin and many other states the grandparents of a baby born to a teenager are responsible for the financial support of the child. Remember parents are not needed if their teenage daughter needs contraceptives or abortion. Faced with such hypocrisy, the parents job is to instill in their teenagers mind what is not taught in sex ed classes, i.e. reason not to engage in sex, reason not to get pregnant, etc. At the same time, they should divert their energies to some productive activities like community work, sports, character growth, or Sunday schools. Another role of parents is to help their children make the right decisions.

In Islam anything which leads to wrong is also considered wrong. Therefore parents should control the music children are listening to or the TV program they are watching, the magazines they are reading, and the clothes (which may provoke desire in the opposite sex) they are wearing. While group social activity should be permitted with supervision, dating should not be allowed. When American teenagers start dating, sex is on their mind.

In fact during a recent survey, 25% of college freshman boys responded by saying that if they have paid for the food and the girl does not go all the way, they have a right to force her to have sex. Many of the rapes occur at the end of the date and are not reported. Anything which breaks down sexual inhibition and loss of self-control i.e. alcohol, drugs, parking, petting or just being together for two members of the opposite sex in a secluded place should not be allowed for Muslim teenagers. Kissing and petting is preparing the body for sex. The body can be brought to a point of no return.

In summary Muslim parents should teach their children that they are different from non-Muslims in their value system and way of life. Having a feeling and love in your heart for someone of the opposite sex is different and beyond control, while expression of the same through sex is entirely different and should be under control. Muslim children should be told that they don't drink alcohol, eat pork, take drugs, and they don't have to engage in pre-marital sex either.

ISLAMIC CONCEPT OF SEXUALITY

Islam recognizes the power of sexual need, but the subject is discussed in the Quran and the saying of Prophet Muhammad (☙) in a serious manner, in regard to marital and family life. Parents should familiarize themselves with this body of knowledge.

SAYINGS OF PROPHET MUHAMMAD (☙)

1. "When one of you have sex with your wife, it is a rewarded act of charity." The Companions were surprised and said, "But we do it purely out of our desire. How can it be counted as charity?" The Prophet replied, "If you had done it with a forbidden woman, it would have been counted as a sin, but if you do it in legitimacy, it is counted as charity."

2. "Let not one of you fall upon his wife like a beast falls. It is more appropriate to send a message before the act."

3. "Do not divulge the secrets of your sex life with your wife to another person nor describe her physical feature to anyone."

CONCEPT OF ADULTERY IN ISLAM

God says in the Quran, *"Do not go near to adultery. Surely it is a shameful deed and evil, opening roads (to other evils)"* (17:32). *"Say, 'Verily, my Lord has prohibited the shameful deeds, be it open or secret, sins and trespasses against the truth and reason'"* (7:33). *"Women impure are for men impure, and men impure are for women impure and women of purity are for men of purity, and men of purity are for women of purity"* (24:26). Prophet Muhammad (ﷺ) has said in many place that adultery is one of the three major sins. However the most interesting story is that of a young man who went to the Prophet and asked for permission to fornicate because he could not control himself. The Prophet dealt with him with reasoning and asked him if he would approve of someone else having illegal sex with his mother, sister, daughter or wife. Each time the man said 'no'. Then the Prophet replied that the woman with whom you plan to have sex is also somebody's mother, sister, daughter or wife. The man understood and repented. The Prophet prayed for his forgiveness.

Adultery is a crime not against one person but against the whole of society. It is a violation of marital contract. 50% of all first time marriages in this country result in divorce in two years and the main reason for divorce is the adultery of one of the partners. Adultery, which includes both pre-marital and extra marital sex, is an epidemic in this society. Nobody seems to listen to the Bible which says frequently, "Thou shall not commit adultery." The Quranic approach is, "Do not approach adultery."

What does it mean that not only is illegal sex prohibited, but anything which leads to illegal sex is also illegal? These things include dating, free mixing of the sexes, provocative dress, nudity, obscenity and pornography. The dress code both for men and women is to protect them from temptation and desires by on lookers who may lose self-control and fall into sin. *"Say to the believing men that they should lower their gaze and guard their modesty; that will make for greater purity, and God is well acquainted with all they do. And say to the believing woman that they should lower their gaze, and guard their modesty"* (24:30-31).

CONCEPT OF MARRIAGE IN ISLAM

Islam recognizes the strong sexual urge and desire for reproduction. Thus Islam encourages marriage as a legal sexual means and as a shield from immorality (sex without commitment). In Islam the marriage of a man and woman is not just a financial and legal living arrangement, not even just for reproduction, but providing a total commitment to each other, a contract witnessed by God. Love and joy of companionship is a part of the commitment. A married couple assumes a new social status and responsibility for himself, his wife and his children and for the community. The Quran says, *"Among His signs is that He created consorts for you from among yourself, so that you may find tranquillity with them, and (He) set love and compassion between you. Verily in this are signs for people who reflect"* (30:21).

SAYINGS OF PROPHET MUHAMMAD (ﷺ)

"Marriage is my tradition. He who rejects my tradition is not of me" (Bukhari, Muslim).

"Marriage is half of religion. The other half is being Godfearing" (Tabarani, Hakim).

In Islam there is no fixed rule as to the age of marriage. It is becoming fashionable for young Muslim men not to marry until they have completed their education, have a job, or reached age 26-30 or more. Similarly young Muslim girls say they want to marry after age 24. Why? When asked, they say, "I am not ready for it." Not ready for what? Don't they have normal sexual desire? If the answer is yes, then they have only one of the two choices a) marry or b) postpone sex (abstinence until they marry). The Quran says, *"Let those who find not the where withal for marriage, to keep them selves chaste till God find them the means from His Grace"* (24:33).

The Prophet said, "Those of you who own the means should marry, otherwise should keep fasting for it curbs desires" (Ibn Massoud). The Western reason for delaying marriage is different than ours. When I suggested this to one of my sexually active young female patients, she bluntly said, "I don't want to sleep with the same guy every night."

ROLE OF MUSLIM PARENTS
AND MUSLIM ORGANIZATIONS

I am not proposing that all Muslim youth be married at age 16. But I must say that youth should accept the biological instinct and make decisions which will help to develop a more satisfied life devoted to having a career rather than spending time in chasing (or dreaming about) the opposite sex. Parents should help their sons and daughters in selection of their mate using Islamic practice as a criteria and not race, color or wealth. They should encourage them to know each other in a supervised setting. The community organization has several roles to play.

a) To provide a platform for boys and girls to see and know each other without any intimacy.

b) Offer premarital educational courses to boys and girls over 18 separately to prepare them for the role of father and husband and of mother and wife. The father has a special role, mentioned by Prophet Muhammad (ﷺ), "One who is given by God, a child, he should give it a beautiful name, should give him or her education, and training and when he or she attains puberty, he should see to it that he or she is married. If the father does not arrange their marriage after puberty, and the boy or girl is involved in sin, the responsibility of that sin will lie with the father"

MARRIAGE OF MUSLIM GIRLS IN THE USA

Marriage of Muslim girls in this country is becoming a problem. I was not surprised to read the letter of a Muslim father in a national magazine. He complained that in spite of his doing his best in teaching Islam to his children, his college-going daughter announced that she is going to marry a non-Muslim boy whom she met in college.

As a social scientist I am more interested in the analysis of the events. To be more specific, why would a Muslim girl prefer a non-Muslim boy over a Muslim? The following reasons come to mind:

• She is opposed to and scared of arranged marriages. She should be told that not all arranged marriages are bad ones and that 50% of all love marriages end up in a divorce in this country. Arranged marriages can be successful if approved by both the boy and girl. That is, they need to be a party to the arrangement. I am myself opposed to the blind arranged marriage.

• Muslim boys are not available to her to make a choice. While parents have no objection or cannot do anything about non-Muslim boys with whom she talks or socializes at school or college for forty hours a week, she is not allowed to talk to a Muslim boy in the mosque or in a social gathering. If she does, they frown at her or even accuse her of having a loss character. As a Muslim boy put it, "If I grow up knowing only non-Muslim girls, why do my parents expect me to marry a Muslim one?"

• Some Muslim boys do not care for Muslim girls. On the pretext of missionary work after marriage, they get involved with non-Muslim girls because of their easy availability. Muslim parents who also live with an inferiority complex do not mind their son marrying an American girl of European background but they would object if he marries a Muslim girl of a different school of Islamic thought (Shiah/Sunni) or different tribe like Punjabi, Sunni, Pathan, Arab vs. non-Arab, Afro-American vs. immigrant, or different class, Syed vs. non-Syed. Both the parents and the body should be reminded that the criteria for choosing a spouse that was given by the Prophet Muhammad (ﷺ) was not wealth nor color but Islamic piety.

• She may have been told that early marriage, that is, age 18 or less, is taboo and that she should wait until the age of 23 or 25. According to statistics, 80% of American girls, while waiting to get settled in life and married, engage freely in sex with multiple boyfriends. However, this option is not available to Muslim girls. Every year nearly one million teenage girls in this country who think that they are not ready for marriage, get pregnant. By the age of 24 when a Muslim girl decides that she is ready for marriage, it may be too large for her. If she reviews the matrimonial ad section in Islamic magazines, she will quickly notice that the boys of the age group of 25 to 30 are looking for girls from 18 to 20 year age group. They may wrongfully assume that an older girl may not be a virgin.

• She may also carry a wrong notion not proven scientifically that marrying healthy cousins may cause congenital deformities in her offspring.

Thus, unless these issues are addressed, many Muslim girls in the US may end up marrying a non-Muslim or remain unmarried.

CURRICULUM FOR ISLAMIC SEX EDUCATION

Islamic sex ed should be taught at home starting at an early age. Before giving education about anatomy and physiology, the belief in the Creator should be well established. As Dostoevsky put it, "Without God, everything is possible," meaning that the lack of belief or awareness of God gives an OK for wrongdoing.

A father should teach his son and a mother should teach her daughter. In the absence of a willing parent, the next best choice should be a Muslim male teacher (preferably a physician) for boys and a Muslim female

teacher (preferably a physician) for a girl at the Islamic Sunday school.
The curriculum should be tailored according to age of the child and classes be held separately. Only pertinent answers to a question should be given. By this I mean that if a five year old asks how he or she got into mommie's stomach, there is no need to describe the whole act of intercourse. Similarly it is not necessary to tell a fourteen year old how to put on condoms. This might be taught in premarital class just before his or her marriage. A curriculum for sex ed should Include:

    a. Sexual growth and development
        * Time table for puberty
        * Physical changes during puberty
        * Need for family life
    b. Physiology of reproductive system
        * For girls— the organ, menstruation, premenstrual syndrome
        * For boys— the organ, the sex drive
    c. Conception, development of fetus and birth
    d. Sexually transmitted disease (VD/AIDS) (emphasize the Islamic aspect)
    e. Mental, emotional and social aspects of puberty
    f. Social, moral and religious ethics
    g. How to avoid peer pressure

SEX EDUCATION AFTER MARRIAGE

This essay is not intended to be a sex manual for married couples, although I may write such someday. I just wanted to remind the reader of a short verse in the Quran and then elaborate. The verse is, *"They are your garments, and you are their garments"* (2:187).

Husbands and wives are described as garments for each other. A garment is very close to our body, so they should be close to each other. A garment protects and shields our modesty, so they should do the same to each other. Garments are put on anytime we like, so should they be available to each other anytime. A garment adds to our beauty, so they should praise and beautify each other.

For husbands I should say that sex is an expression of love and one without the other is incomplete. One of your jobs is to educate your wife in matters of sex especially in your likes and dislikes and do not compare her to other women.

For wives I want to say that a man's sexual needs are different than a women's. Instead of being a passive recipient of sex, try to be an active partner. He is exposed to many temptations outside the home. Be available to please him and do not give him a reason to make a choice between you and hellfire.

SELECTED REFERENCES

Annual Report of Children's Defense Fund. *Northside Topics.* January, 1988.

"Children Having Children." *Time Magazine.* December 9, 1985.

Curran, J. Report of Center for Disease Control. *Indianapolis Star,* June 14, 1988.

Dracula of Hormones. *Newsweek Magazine.* November 25, 1985.

Elam, A. and V. G. Ray. "Sexually Related Trauma: A Review." *Annals of Emergency Medicine,* May, 1986, vol. 15:5, pp. 576-584.

Gordon, S. and I. R. Dickman. "Sex Education—My Parent's Role," Public Affairs Pamphlet No. 549. Published by Public Affairs Committee, 381 Park Ave. South, New York, NY 10016.

Hatcher, Adams J. "Solving Teenage Pregnancy." *Medical Aspects of Human Sexuality.* March, 1980, pp. 10-23.

Marvin, S. "How Adults Could Have Helped Me." *Parade Magazine,* (Supplement to Indianapolis Star) August 21, 1988, pp. 4-7.

Mast, C. K. "How to Say No to Sex." *Medical Aspects of Human Sexuality.* September, 1988, pp. 26-32.

Mast, C. K. *Sex Respect: The Option of True Sexual Freedom.* Bradley, Il: Respect Inc., 1986, p. 41.

Muslim, Bukhari. *Collection of Hadith.*

Nelson, C. A. *A Cancer Journal For Clinicians.* American Cancer Society. November-December, 1984.

Report On Sex Education. *Time Magazine.* November. 24, 1986.

Report on Teens: Sex Attitude Survey by Eight National Evangelical Churchs. *Indianapolis Star.* February 2, 1988.

Richard, D. "Teenage Pregnancy and Sex Education in the Schools: What Works And What Does Not Work," San Antonio Pregnancy Center, 1986, p. 6.

Stroud. "Stop Pornographic Rock." *Newsweek Magazine.* May 6, 1985.

Time Magazine. February 4, 1985, p. 85.

"What's Gone Wrong With Teen Sex?" *People Magazine.* April 13, 1987.

Williams, R. H. "Effects of Melatonins in Humans." *Textbook of Endocrinology,* 6th Ed., p. 628.

Zamichow, N. Teenage Sex. *Ladies Home Journal,* October 1986, pp. 138-205.

HIV Today and Tomorrow

Worldwide, more than 12 million people are infected with HIV. The great majority live in Africa, south of the Sahara. But as the inset shows, Asia is poised to become the plague's next epicenter.

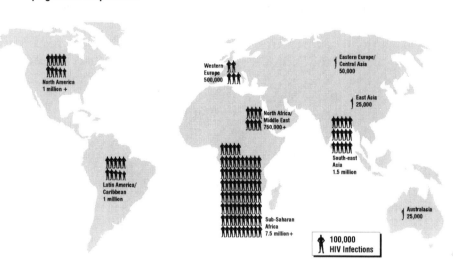

2
WHERE DO WE GO FROM HERE?
SHAHID ATHAR

S tandard sex education today "tends to be morally bankrupt. It begins with a biological description of sexual function and fertility (known in the trade as the organ concert) and it ends with indoctrination in conception, abortion and venereal disease. Basic to this pedagogy is the belief that youngsters will not accept moral ideals and should at least (or at most) be helped to cut their losses."

Father James Burtchaell

Raising children these days is not an easy job. No wonder many Americans do not want to get married, and if they do, do not want to have children. Each child needs the individual attention of both parents, and time, a most precious gift that we are sometimes unable to find for our children. Parents who were themselves raised either in a different country or in a different generation, where peer pressure was different, have more difficulty in raising today's children. They also do not get much help from television or the school system. What kinds of suggestions do I have for them.

First of all, I do not like using the phrase, 'setting limits'. No one likes

21

to take orders these days in this free society. A better term would be educated guidelines for both parents and youth. Even better is the term 'informed consent', the kind we use in medicine before asking a patient to agree to a procedure or a test. Once a person is informed of the consequences of right and wrong, then he or she can make an intelligent decision. Unfortunately, smaller children are not able to make that decision for themselves, so parents will have to do it for them until the child reaches the age of maturity.

Children have a right to be treated as people, in an environment that is conducive for their growth and maturity and to become useful citizens. Children have a right to love, care, discipline and protection from their parents. Children have a right to receive education and financial protection for the future.

Parents have a right to receive love, respect and affection from their children. Parents have a right to educate and discipline their children. Parents have a right to know about their children and monitor other influences affecting them. Parents have a right to say no to unusual financial and other demands of children.

The next question is, "Why set limits or give guidelines? Why not let the boat sail without a sail in an uncharted sea?" If it does, most likely this boat will end up at a destination where it never wanted to be. Thus, not only do we need to prepare for the present but also for the future. All those children who are adults now, who were reared with discipline, appreciate what their parents did when they were children in terms of discipline, although it appeared at that time that the discipline was too tough."

The next question becomes, "In what areas should we set limits? The most important area is time management. Children, as well as adults, waste too much time in watching TV, listening to music, talking on the telephone, and other unnecessary activities. They must realize that whatever time they are wasting, they are taking it away from some more useful work like homework or housework. Therefore, they must set limits and assign priorities with respect to their time management. Their health comes first. Next comes homework and education and then time spent in improving interpersonal relationships.

Another question is who should set the limit? Traditionally, it is seen as the father's role and sometimes the mother's role, an elder brother for a younger brother, or an elder sister for a younger sister. On the other hand, the truth is the one who is better qualified and more experienced should set the limits for the one who is less qualified and less experienced.

In terms of religion, the one with stronger faith and righteous deeds should set limits for the one who has less, regardless of age. Sometimes it is seen that the parents are less practicing Muslims than the children themselves. In that case, the children should advise the parents. Teachers have a much greater role to play. However, the limits should be taken in the light of permission and responsibility from God.

SOME SUGGESTIONS TO PARENTS

Choose a good neighborhood school. Know the teachers personally and interact with them. Neglected children expose themselves to various abuses. Supervise their homework.

Watch TV with your children and select good educational and entertainment programs. Comment on the negative aspects of the program. Cut down TV time to less than twelve hours on weekdays and twenty-two hours on weekends. Encourage outdoor activity. Encourage them to read newspapers and good magazines

Growing children may not obey an order, but they will do things out of love and respect for their parents. Love and respect on a mutual basis is our best weapon against all the negative influences.

Parental love should be unconditional and not based on their achievements. Love should not be confused with permissiveness or overlooking a child's faults. Pointing out faults of the child should not diminish the love by the parents.

Children are not born knowing all the rights or wrongs in social norm. They need clear guidelines about good and bad behavior. The greatest effect is the parent's attitude, example and behavior rather than words. Parents should set the same standards for themselves as they set for their children and share with them information of all kinds whether related to the outside world or inside the family. It is not the knowledge which hurts but the lack of it, or misuse of it, which causes problems.

Parents should help children to make appropriate decisions and be responsible for them. Younger children can only make decisions about the present (i.e., what clothes to wear that day), but older children can make decisions that may affect their future, under parental guidance (i.e., selection of school, college and career). Children should be taught to share household work, keep their desk and room clean, and how to handle their 'own' money. Let them spend all their money and suffer from the lack of it.

The overprotective and anxious parent cannot raise a confident child ready to deal with the real world. This child will feel danger everywhere. While the child has to be supervised, he or she does not need the physical presence of the parent all the time. They should raise a strong child. The parent who cannot say no to a child spoils the child. This child will make unreasonable demands and put on a manipulative show. The parents have to discipline themselves in order to discipline their children. Parents who take sides in sibling rivalry encourage jealousy and hate. They should not prefer boys over girls, fair complexions over dark ones, the honor roll over an average student.

Neither party can influence the other unless they communicate. Find a time and place to talk to your children. Children are sometimes in a 'bad mood' upon returning from school, loaded with homework. The best time to have a chat is during breakfast and evening dinner. During this time, the parent can inform the child of all the good things he or she did that day and ask the child the same and share his or her problems.

When you do argue, do it patiently, one person speaking at a time. Be specific and separate emotion from facts. Speak in a low tone, Screaming decreases the intake of the message.

Practice active listening from each other's view, even if you don't agree. Refrain from sarcasm, name calling, humiliating, pointing your finger, etc. Encourage each other even in areas of shortcoming, rather than making fun or making a negative remark, i.e., if the child brings a B-report, then instead of, "I doubt you will ever improve or pass your exam," say, "B is better than C," and "I am sure you are talented enough to do better. May I help you in the areas that you have difficulties in at school?"

The purpose of giving them chores is to keep them busy as well as to teach them responsibility. Initially it may be boring but eventually will become routine. The assignment should be according to age and not the sex of the child. However, children should not be forced into doing things, or otherwise they will rebel. By the same token, they should not be penalized for mistakes. The best payment for a job is a smile, hug, thank you or praising the child in the presence of others, rather than money. While it may be all right to give an allowance, it should not be tied to the job.

SETTING LIMITS IN GENDER INTERACTION

In Islam intimate mixing of youth and adults of opposite sexes by themselves is not permitted for social reasons. Thus we oppose dating and all such activities. Nevertheless, there is a need for Muslim boys and girls over eighteen to get to know each other so that when they attain the age for marriage, hopefully, they will choose a Muslim spouse. This can be done in a supervised setting whether during a community function, mosque, ISNA or MYNA convention.

Talking to a non-*mahram* for business or religious reasons is permitted in Islam. Both boys and girls, men and women, should lower their gaze, dress appropriately and talk in a business manner and not in a seductive way. The right of God is that He should be believed in, He should be worshiped and He should be obeyed. Thus, if we set limits and discipline ourselves, the reward is immense and includes not only success in this world but also in the hereafter with the pleasure of God.

3
ROLE OF THE MUSLIM
PHYSICIAN IN SEX EDUCATION
EL TIGANI ADAM HAMMAD

Today's sex eduction is " one of the most devastating things that can possibly happen to any society and it certainly has overwhelmed our society. For over one hundred years, established psychological precepts, which have repeatedly been substantiated by clinical observations, reveal two important facts concerning human sexuality. The first is that life-sustaining human sexual needs can only be fulfilled in an-affectionate, monogamous, heterosexual relationship. Sex educators do not stress this fact enough. The second salient psychoanalytic fact is that, in humans, unlike in any other creatures, three phases of sexual development occur before mature adult sexuality is reached. The public school courses given during each of these phases cause great harm to student and society in general."

Melvin Anchell,
The New American,
May 11,1987

Sex education is only one facet of the multitude of social changes in Western societies that successfully transformed societal attitudes towards previously strongly accepted and adhered to basic assumptions and principles. Capital punishment, mercy killing, abortion, homosexuality and legalization of cannabis are further examples where ethical issues and moral judgments seem to lack consistency with time in Western societies. The rationalization of such perpetual attitudinal changes can partly be found in the Freudian concept of the pleasure principle and his interpretation of human behavior as a function of aggression and sexuality. It can partly be explained by a decline in spirituality and a tendency to embrace materialism.

Islam defines the essence of life and rationalizes the creation of the universe simply and explicitly, "*I have created jinn and humankind only that they might worship me*" (51:56). "Life here is a vehicle to the hereafter." Thus Muslim life is to be based on submission and adherence to the will of God and His instructions. These two contradictory approaches to the perception of life are applicable to any major issue in existence concerning the Muslim and non-Muslim. The choice is left to the individual which way to decide, bearing in mind the implications of his decision and accepting liability for his actions.

WHAT IS SEX EDUCATION?

Schofield writes in his book on promiscuity, "Intercourse and other sexual activities are for pleasure and ought to be encouraged as such...The purpose of sexual intercourse is sexual enjoyment." He continues, "Sex education, if it is to be any good, must help the pupil to adapt to new conditions, new ideas, different ethics, different values...." Thus ethics and values should change to serve the pleasure principle and should do so early in life. The physical, biological, social and psychological aspects of sexual life are taught to children and they are encouraged to practice and experience them at an early age and even before adolescence. It is then only logical to add the subjects of contraception, abortion and pornography to the syllabus in an attempt to avert undesirable consequences. As one child put it, "How do we know we are not to be trapped in a marriage that she wants, but we don't?"

IS THERE SEX EDUCATION IS ISLAM?

Islam comprises a total way of life. Each part of it needs to be seen in the total context. Thus it is hard to take any major issue in life in isolation. Thus sexual life cannot be conceived of without marital and family life and these are all to be considered in relation to other Islamic teachings which regulate and control Muslim behavior.

Ibn al-Quyem in his book, *Prophetic Medicine*, assigned a full chapter to discussing the Islamic attitude to sexual and marital life, the interaction between the spouses, and the permissions and prohibitions concerning sexual intercourse between spouses. Muhammad Qutb in his book, Islam the Misunderstood Religion, discussed the subject in two chapters, one On Islam and Woman and the other, On Islam and Sexual Repression. Reading through the Quran and the Traditions of the Prophet there are many verses and Traditions about the creation of human life, cleanliness and purity, interaction between tile spouses, and mention of sexual intercourse between the spouses. In the explanation of these verses and Traditions, issues did arise, questions were asked and both sexes were involved jointly or separately. The following important points can be made:

1. In Islam sex has always been taken seriously and it should remain so. It is not a subject for fun or mere absolute pleasure. It is never discussed obscenely or subjected to scrutiny. Decency and due respect always characterize the subject.

2. Sex is never discussed in isolation for its sake or mere pleasure. It is always related to marital life and family life. It is is viewed as a superior human relationship subject to strict regulations. Thus sex within a marital relationship is a worship that is rewarded. Outside a marital relationship sex is a punishable sin.

3. Sex is a privacy between the spouses. What goes on is confidential and should not be divulged to outside parties. The human factor in marital and sexual relationship is superior to mere pleasure.

4. Legislation concerning sex is not subject to change by pressure groups or change in social attitudes.

5. Like the rest of Islamic teaching, knowledge about those verses and Traditions on the subject is not age-specific and is not meant to start at a certain age. As the Muslim is learning the Quran and *Sunnah* he or she will come across these teachings.

THE ROLE OF THE MUSLIM PHYSICIAN

Here we have to consider several issues. Why should we concern ourselves with sex education? Why is the question asked at this time? Is sex education such an important issue in Muslim life and Muslim society? Furthermore, who needs sex education? How and when should it be made available? Who should face the problem and provide the service? What are the sources and means of information?

More specific questions are what are the bases of the theoretical principles that apply? What are the problems and dangers of practical application? This multitude of questions reflects my anxieties as a Muslim psychiatrist who puts his faith and fear of God before his career and profession. My fear of committing a sin predates my enthusiasm of doing a successful job.

However, it would be more positive and productive if the answers to these questions were authenticated and qualified so as to stand criticism and confront challenge. The question arises because sex education is part of a package being delivered to Muslims by the Western civilization in an attempt to dismantle them from their basic roots of Islamic life. This package comprises abortion, insurance, contraception, liberal attitudes to alcohol, dress and other anti-Islamic behavior. Unfortunately part of the package has already been delivered, received and well digested. If we are not careful there is worse to come. Nowadays such anti-islamic behaviors and concepts are not necessarily delivered by missionaries and foreign anti-islamic agents. Muslims professing to be liberalists, reformists or saviours are doing the job.

HOW CAN A MUSLIM PHYSICIAN HANDLE THE PROBLEM?

Do we really have a role in sex education? What are our theoretical principles and means of application? What are the ethical and moral issues? The chances are there that once in lifetime a consultation may involve a sexual problem. What can we do? The first requirement is a combination of medical knowledge and Islamic orientation. One should know where he stands. The second requirement is setting limits on moral and ethical principles. And the third requirement is a knowledge of the patient and his or her religious and moral orientation. If these requirements are satisfied then one may be facing one of three situations:

a. Sex education

b. Sexual deviation

c. Sexual dysfunction

If any of these situations arise outside a marital relationship, I can hardly see myself helping somebody to continue such a relationship. It is a sin to help abominations. If there is any education for non-marital relationships that would then be to stop them or suppress the desire. One cannot help these people at the expense of religious convictions and legislature. We cannot sacrifice Islam for those who move towards moral degradation or try to avoid the legal responsibility for their non-islamic sexual behavior. Within a marital relationship how much can we indulge in sex education? One can consider situations where spouses come for help but one cannot go out of his or her way to preach sex education. Of course people need to know the dangers of venereal disease, rape, illegitimacy and criminal abortion but this should not by necessity be exclusively for the medical profession to preach.

WHAT DO WE HAVE TO TEACH?

The Muslim doctor needs to understand thoroughly all that the Quran has mentioned pertaining to sex and all that the Traditions of the Prophet included concerning conjugal rights and how spouses should treat each other concerning those conjugal rights. The Quran says, "S*o let man consider fools what he is created." "He is created from a gushing fluid that issues from between the loins and ribs."* It goes on to say, *"Did We not create you from a base fluid which We laid up in a safe abode for a known term. Thus We arranged. How excellent is Our arranging."*

This theme keeps recurring in the Quran and is always related to other teachings. *"Verily We created the human being from a product of wet earth, then placed him as a drop in a safe lodging, then fashioned We the drop a clot, then fashioned We the clot a little lump, then fashioned We the little lump bones, then clothed the bones with flesh, and then produced it as another creation—so blessed be God, the best of Creators."*

In other chapters the Quran says, *"Then lo! On the Day of Resurrection you are raised."* And, *"There is enough here for Muslims to reflect on—creation, death, resurrection."* And, *"They question you concerning menstruation. Say it is an illness so refrain from women during menstruation and do not approach them until they are purified. Once they purify themselves then enjoy them from where God has instructed you.*

Truly God loves the repenters and those who care for purity" (4:222-223). *"Your women are a tilth for you (to cultivate) so enjoy your tilth the way you wish and make an introduction for yourselves..."*

What more details do we need to know to fulfill this human instinct. The closest you can come to details is what happened between Joseph and Zulayka. *"And she approached him, she in whose house he was and she bolted the doors and said I am ready for you. He said I seek refuge in God—Lo! He is my Lord Who perfected my resort. Wrongdoers never prosper. She verily desired him and he desired her but he saw the sign of his Lord. Thus it was that We might ward off from him evil and lewdness. Lo! He was of Our chosen slaves and they raced to the door and she tore his shirt from behind."*

The Prophet (ﷺ) says, "The best of you is the one who is best to his family." He also said, "Beloved to me of your world are pleasant scents and women." He once told the Companions, "And there is a reward for what you deposit in the womb of your wife." They said, "Oh Messenger of God, the one of us satisfies his desire and gets a reward for that." He answered, "What if he deposits it in a prohibited womb? Isn't he going to sin?" So if he deposits it in a permitted womb there is a reward for him.

But at the same time he instructed his Companions not to divulge what goes on between them in private as husband and wife. He simulated that happening to a devil making love to a she-devil. He also instructed women not to describe the particulars of their female friends to their husbands as if they can see the woman described. This is to avoid masturbation in fantasy and abominations.

The physician may have more to offer in cases of sexual dysfunction within a marital relationship. He may find physical or organic pathology that needs correction. He may detect psychological factors having an impact on the sexual relationship. The physician has still to set limits to how deep and far he can go. The decency and virtue of marital bondage and privacy of such a relationship need not be obscenely dissected and divulged to a third party, particularly if he or she be of the opposite sex, and here the need for same sex therapists becomes important. Do we really need to worry that much about sexual problems? Do we have so many of them as to warrant explicit discussions? A more general answer is that in a practicing Muslim society we should not expect to face the same problems as Western societies. Female Muslim physicians in a Muslim society need not worry about handling overt and obscene sexual problems. One main reason to believe this assumption is that the Quran and the *Sunnah* should be the framework for Muslim life and thus shape and fashion the behavior and attitudes of Muslims. As the children are brought up they will have an Islamic orientation to marital life and sex education is then part of that education rather than a separate and major issue in isolation. We do not need to take sex as an issue and introduce it into the education of children. We need to introduce to them the Quran and *Sunnah* in toto. If they can care for their Islamic character other issues will take care of themselves. Virtue breeds virtue and vice breeds vice. Those who enjoy life as a whole should hope to enjoy their marital life both emotionally and physically and should not lack the means to do so.

REFERENCES

Ibn al-Quyem al-Jawziyah, *al-Tibb al-Nabawi*.

Qutb, Muhammad. *Islam, the Misunderstood Religion.*

Sahih Muslim.

Schofield, M. *Promiscuity*. Publishers Victor Gollallcz Limited, London, 1976.

4
SEX ROLES IN MUSLIM FAMILIES IN THE US

MAHMOUD ABU SAUD

ORIGIN OF THE FAMILY: BIOLOGICAL FACTOR

U nless sex education addresses "values, morality, deferment of gratification, and goals, it is incomplete and potentially dangerous."

> Donald Ian Macdonald.
> An Approach to the Prevention of
> Teenage Pregnancy,
> *Public Health Report*,
> July/August 1987

Sociologists give different definitions of the family institution to which we shall refer later. However, and for the purpose of this essay, we shall consider that the basic biological coupling of a male and a female is an essential element to constitute a family, as homosexuality does not exist in nature.

THE CELL

Biologically speaking, all living things are made of just two kinds of cells: eukaryotes and prokaryotes. The first ones are those cells which have nuclei and multiply by mating or marriage. The second, the prokaryotes, are those which have no nuclei and accordingly are unicellular, multiplying by division. Each cell has its hereditary traits and carries its information in DNA (deoxyribonucleic acid). ". . . two extremely long strands of it, wrapped around each other in a double helix.'"[1] It is of fascinating interest to know that only the eukaryotes are "capable of making up the bodies of the marvels of creation—those with hearts, lungs, kidneys and brains."[2] The prokaryotes are parasitic by nature and are deadly enemies of the eukaryotes who eat them up or destroy them with their enzymatic secretions. Human organisms are no more than the sum of their cells functioning together.

Sex, a word for the exchange of genetic material, requires two organisms to come together and reproduce. Though there are some organisms that can reproduce without sex, such as some bacteria, their progeny are doomed to be identical to the parent without variation or susceptibility to evolution. Evolution needs genetic variety which can only be realized by means of ever new combinations of genes of heterosexual cells—the eukaryotes.

Before exploring the functioning of cells as constituents of human males and females, it is of great interest to know that cells themselves are the product of atoms. Atoms follow an eternal strict code of behavior as if they had some sort of consciousness that brings them together in a highly organized manner. They form molecules in extraordinarily geometric forms; molecules make "tissues that become the organs that inexorably build the organism.. Every molecule has its own distinct properties by virtue of the atoms that make it up and. . . life has its properties by virtue of the molecule used in constructing living organisms."[3] All living organisms, including bacteria, must use nucleic acid organized into genes for reproduction. The genes are the true carriers of all hereditary traits and properties of the offspring.

Such established elementary knowledge reveals some basic facts of life that concern us in this study. The first fact is that prokaryotes—the unicellular organisms—are parasitic and destructive. They are not capable of evolution and do not constitute any part of our functioning organisms.

The second is that eukaryotes cannot continue to exist without marriage as they multiply by means of coupling. Their union is the basis of evolution to the better through a process of natural selection. They are endowed with a gift to choose the fittest from among themselves and thus genetically improve.

The third is that all molecules belong in their first origin to the atom, which by virtue of its nature does not exist without union. The components of the atom: the protons, the neutrons, and the electrons are likewise bound to unite.

Thus, marriage is simply a law of existence, an inherent property ingrained in our cells and constitution without which we cannot continue to live or evolve. In each cellular marriage there must be the male and the female, or the positive which gives in mating to the negative which takes. In the world of the cell, which is our world, everything goes on progressing in meticulous order. Order defines the cell as the cell defines life. "Before there was life, there had to be a system. . . there has to be order. . . it is life. . . Death is disorder."[4]

HUMAN BIOLOGY

Much has been discovered about the cell, its composition, its functioning and its reproduction yet nobody has been able to guess how the first cell came into being. The eukaryotes, as mentioned before, are highly organized and highly specialized cells that build our body and, in fact, bring us into life. Every cell is composed of several layers above layers of molecules separated by membranes, and in its middle there is the nucleus ringed by double membrane. The nucleus holds the genes—the ultimate dictators of the cell—wound into the coils of chromosomes.

Humans reproduce through the union of a male and a female cell, exactly as any other offspring is reproduced. When fertilization (union or mating) takes place, a new cell is formed and the sex, together with the physical structure, including the brain, are determined by the genes united in the new cell. Both males and females have the same basis of a chromosome (X). But from the very beginning, if this basis is coupled with one (X) chromosome or more, the offspring is a female. If the basis is coupled with one chromosome (Y) or more, it is a male.

Once the new cell is "born," it starts functioning on its own, activated by its inherent power administered by the new set of genes, and is called, in this early stage, a zygote. Soon after inception, male embryos secrete a predominant hormone called androgen, while female ones secrete estrogen, and later on the female hormones: the progesterone and the prolactin. The growth of the embryo, whether male or female, follows the same laws of growth: the reproduction of the specialized cells continues building up our different organs, without any deviation except for hormonal secretions. By the time the child is born, he or she has already been influenced by the most active hormones which affect the functioning of the brain.

The human brain is one of the greatest wonders of creation. In its lower part, there is a small zone called the "limbic system," composed of structures which are involved in both human emotion and motivation. One of these structures, named amygdala, is among the major brain parts responsible for our behavior, as it affects some endocrinal secretions, especially those touching upon our sexual dispositions. Moreover, "the cortex also feeds it (the limbic system) with condensed indications of cortical activity, including categorized representations of the state of the external world. It appraises and evaluates the activities of (the upper brain —system). . . and balances current priorities with regard to short term and long-term needs of the organism and the selection and evaluation of different integrative activities."[5]

It is well-established that the structure called "hypothalamus" of the limbic system is pre-natally formed and becomes indelibly 'sex-typed' through the action of sex-hormones, thereby permanently pre-disposing the animal to male or female physiological and behavioral responses. In most animals this critical period of hormone action is thought to occur prenatally and thereafter be immutable. "This irrevocable hormonal sex-typing of the nervous system has the most far-reaching implications for sex differences in human behavior."[6] This means that from the earliest days of conception the new fertilized cell or zygote our brain starts its formation, disposition and mode of functioning.

When born, an infant carries within himself or herself its own particular way of thinking, imagination, motivation and manner of evaluation.

Even among individuals of the same sex, there are genetic inherent differences due to the differences in the rates of flow of hormones into the brain. Chromosome (Y) is responsible for the male hormones androgen, which are associated with what the psychologists call the "aggressive" tendency, meaning that type of behavior which is generally characterized by a direct and overt reaction, competitive acumen, and long-term evaluation and perception. The term implies, also some final and actual aggressive action which, unless well disciplined, would cause destructive consequences. As a matter of biological fact, such hormones in a male embryo rely on a hormone called "gonadal" which accounts for the behavioral differences between the two sexes and which is thought to influence the behavioral decisions issued by the brain.

In the female, sex hormones are responsible for the menstrual flow which is directly regulated by the key female hormones: estrogen and progesterone. Less secretion of these hormones causes menstruation usually accompanied by a state of discomfort, inhibition, and often gloomy attitudes. It is believed that the hormonal input in this case affects the functioning of the brain of the female, inhibiting or reviving her emotional state. Biologists emphasize the fact that the natural disposition in human is to a female system (X) unless broken by the male chromosome (Y) causing production of the male hormone: androgen.[7]

Aggression—as previously defined—is the product of the testestrone hormone, androgen, a hormone that exists in the supra-renal glands of both sexes but, of course, in widely varied quantities. Aggression in women is mostly due to an overdose of this hormone, unless the woman is suffering from some societal trauma. A violently aggressive man is likewise greatly motivated by an extra dose of androgen. If such a man is given estrogen, he would calm down in most cases and develop a new more docile behavior. In transsexuality, the individual who chooses to become a female undergoes surgical intervention and female hormone therapy without which femininity cannot take its usual course. Hormones, in such circumstances, are necessary to build up the breast, to stimulate sexual desires, to eliminate profuse facial and body hair, etc. Once the new female is given such hormonal treatment, her limbic system functions accordingly: The maternal instinct becomes greatly felt, the desire for talking more becomes more persistent, the feminine emotionality supersedes rationality, and the lachrymatal glands secrete more profuse tears during emotional stress. Nothing, perhaps, can be more convincing of the biological dichotomy than maternity. Weitz writes, "Animal evidence does support the concept of the maternal instinct, in that female sex hormones such as estrogen, progesterone and prolactin seem to be implicated in the ontogeny of maternal behavior."[8] The same author relates the experiment of the monkey-mother who killed its newly born babies when given androgen and the motherly monkey-father who cared for the babies after receiving female hormones. Nowhere in the animal kingdom do fathers assume the basic role of caring for the newly born offspring.[9]

A female child is born with a maternal instinct: she distinctly feels a strong interest in children and this explains why girls prefer to play with dolls. It has been established that girls with an excess of prenatal androgen "do seem to show less interest in infants than normal girls,"[10] and obviously more than normal boys. The maternity behavior is mainly characterized by tenderness, affective bonds, self-preservation, protectiveness, and self-identification with the child.

To conclude, one can safely say that, "Sexual behavior of an individual, and thus gender role, are not neutral and without initial direction at birth. Nevertheless, sexual predisposition is only a potentiality setting limits to a pattern that is greatly modifiable by ontogenetic experience."[11] In other words, the ontogeny (i.e. the biological development of the individual organism) asserts that a female is born with a maternal instinct carrying genetic predispositions different from those of a male. It is of interest to note that there is differential treatment of children by parents according to their sex. Mothers are more inclined to tolerate boys and girls, while fathers are more tolerant towards girls than towards boys. This phenomenon prevails among humans and some primates and is quite conspicuous among monkeys.

SOCIALIZATION FACTORS

"Conspiracy theories of history, which seem to imply that men have kept women down over the centuries through some collective act of will, do not merit serious consideration."[12] There is no doubt that our physiological functioning is affected by our psychological and societal conditions and that biology, psychology and society have contributed to the present sex roles in their different grades and limits. It is rather impossible to separate the biological factor from the societal. Yet, one has to take into serious consideration that there is a definite predisposition in each sex that takes place in the embryo and the fetus. This prenatal conditioning cannot be due to any societal agent, but most probably can be a major cause of societal differential treatment of the sexes. When parents give a doll to their daughter, they are aware of her instinctive motherly feeling and they are responding to her instinctive desires. Instinctive urges can be mollified, re-oriented and mitigated, but never nullified or totally wiped out. To suppress such urges is to cause more harm than good to the individual and to ignore them is to push the child in a wrong way where he or she tries to fulfill the desires by any means, legitimate or illegitimate, socially acceptable or unacceptable.

Socialization agents, namely: the parents, the school, the peers and the social symbols of the sexes, are supposed to be, and in fact should be, factors of disciplining the instinctive behavior. Our basic sexual desires should be satisfied by marriage and not by adultery and fornication. Our instinctive need for security should be met by honorable work and lawful gain and not by theft and violence. Even our innate instinct implanted in the eukaryotes for evolving to the better must be encouraged through a proper education leading to a feeling of self-esteem and elation. Failing this, the individual would resort to unhealthy and even anti-social practices to feel the importance of his ego he or she may develop the bad habits of lying, boasting, or even killing. Any infringement upon instincts is a violation of a natural law of life that conduces to masochism, narcissism, schizophrenia and the rest of the psychotic ailments.

The family has a lasting effect on sex roles as most of the individual's latent behavior is basically formulated in the first seven or eight years of childhood. The major role of parents relates to the child's identification where affective bonds, mechanism of modeling and cognitive categorization should be carefully observed. Here the question generally raised by the "libs" is whether parents should or should not differentiate in their treatment between males and females. Many of them believe that they should not heed the sex and thus should treat both the boy and the girl as if they were of the same sex. They allege that any differentiation at this early stage leads to some category of inferiority complex in the girl and to a bias in favor of the boy. There is enough evidence in everyday life that supports such allegations. However, any fair mind can easily see that it is not the differentiation, per se, that causes such inhibition in the girl, if only because differentiation occurs in families which have girls and no boys. Every individual child is different from others and should accordingly be treated differently. What hurts a child is the way parents associate differentiation with sex. If a doll is given to a grid it is not because she is inferior to a boy who was presented with a horse or a gun. Girls would only suffer inhibition and inferiority if the parents treat them as inferior, or if when differentiating between both of them, parents explain the act in preferential language.

Another important factor in socialization is the school infants in nurseries, children in kindergarten and boys and girls in higher age brackets are treated differently in one way or another, in accordance with their sex. In pictures for the very young, in all books and prints, there is always a "he" and a "she." He is tough, daring, exterior-oriented, and somehow aggressive, while she is kind, caring, child-loving, interior oriented, and somehow self preservative. Then, there are the great differentiation in students' activities: the boys compete in physically rough and hard sports, participate in political and social discussions, and are expected to excel girls in empirical sciences. On the other hand, girls practice dancing and singing, fight and non-violent sports, domestic arts, and are expected to excel boys in artistic sciences.

Here again differentiation is undeniably conspicuous and while it is in essence compatible with human biology, it is condemned by the "libs." Their plea is always the same: such treatment leads to the development of a feeling of inferiority in the female. It indoctrinates the subconscious mind of the girl with a view to convince her of the conspired falsehood, i.e., the superiority of the male. The "libs" believe that keeping the "traditional roles" of sexes in the school gives an edge to the boy over the girl: he is depicted as the hero, the protector, the leader and even the mastery. This seems to be an exaggeration which has its roots in feminine emotion. In many cases, the slave-mind prevails over the "libs" and is manifested in irrational and perverted behavior.

The staunchest proponent of liberalism cannot deny that the male is created with more muscular strength, that biologically speaking, he is more "aggressive," that his mind is more outwardly inclined, and that he is more free from physiological cyclical effects. The female is created with other excellencies anti-distinctions by virtue of her constitution. Her motherhood instincts, her feminine tenderness and her physiologically receptive aptitude for procreation. These clear facts should induce us to accept, at least, such differentiation that confirm anti correspond with the distinct natural characteristics of each sex. It follows that there must be differentiation in all schools to respond to these basic biological divergent requirements.

The so-called peer group effects and the symbolic agents of sex roles are very akin to each other, especially among adults. Clubs of men and women, the distinction in public behavior and the discriminatory treatment of the sexes in many public and social functions do exist in all present societies. One has to admit that some of this differentiation is due to societal factors and/or obsolete inherited tradition. But one cannot also deny that there are genuine irrefutable reasons for differentiation in this field. Despite the equal opportunities open to both sexes in education and public life, women have been active in fields that do not require much "aggressiveness," and where there is a concurrence of biological effect and societal functioning. In such activities there is no reason whatsoever for a woman not to succeed and even excel any man.

SOCIALIZATION VERSUS BIOLOGY

There is evidence that socialization factors, when carried out extensively at an early age, affect the biological functioning of the child. That is how we notice the 'sissy' boy and the 'tomboyish' girl. Also, oversecretion of female hormones in a male would produce the same effect, despite any socialization effort to the contrary. In both cases, the situation becomes unhealthy and the individual suffers from some perversion and could develop trans-sexualism. The correct attitude is obvious: we have to adapt our socialization processes in such a manner that they correspond to our biological functioning. The indelible male and female characteristics installed in our limbic systems as a result of the prenatal hormonal secretions must be the basis of our socialization process. There must be harmony between the act of creation (natural state) and the willful human action. Failing this, a grave imbalance takes place, shaking the personality of the individual to its very roots. Thus, the "libs" claim for identical treatment of males and females in every domain denies the biological constitution of the human mind and body and nullifies masculinity and femininity. Homosexuality, which at present is assuming some prominence in industrialized Western societies, is the product of lopsided thinking and is bound to fail. It is a revolt against the law of creation and will not be allowed to prevail, whatever price humanity may pay for it.

A female must be brought up in a manner that makes her feel proud of her femininity and not ashamed of it. She must be treated with equity but she must not be equated to the male. They are different and can never be equals, as each of them has a domain predestined from his or her conception.

STRUCTURE AND FUNCTION OF THE FAMILY

We have seen that there is no continuity of life without marriage—a union between male and female—and that life is order. Death is entropy or disorder. In Cadmure's words: "Life is mainly to reproduce and to feel."[13] The marriage of cells which constitute our body, brain, and nerves is a highly organized "institution" administered by sophisticated laws and geared by strict discipline. Humans are no more than their cells, and the rule of order and discipline is the essence of their existence. Any violation of this rule is a step towards entropy or self-destruction.

As we live, we reproduce—we marry. Humans learn to live in heterogeneous couples and reproduce within a certain orderly social framework called the "family institution." The word "social" here is not a mere fabrication by man. It is necessarily biological in the sense that one human cell cannot alienate itself from other similar cells. Whenever a group of cells (families) comes together, the necessity for order and discipline becomes incumbent. Hence those who believe that there should be—or even could be—a society of human cells (families) without rules administering the relationships between its individuals, are asking for the impossible, the anti-natural. Such a chaotic grouping does not exist in nature.

Oparin, a Russian biologist, proved that if a collection of molecules (he calls them coacervates) is given a chance to act, they have order. He set a chemical reaction in the solution where these coacervates were floating and found that they formed an inexplicable and unpredicted order: heads outward and tails inward. There was a mystifying difference between the rate of reaction outside and inside the coacervates. According to Oparin, "This difference accounts for the formation of the cell."[14]

Sociologically speaking, a family is operationally defined as "...a special kind of structure whose principals are related to one another through blood ties and/or marital relationships, and whose relatedness is of such a nature as to entail 'mutual expectations' that are prescribed by religion, reinforced by law, and internalized by the individual."[15] This definition takes into account the general aspect of any family and the Islamic point of view. Dr. Abd al-Ati, accordingly specifies the purposes of marriage as:

—a means of emotional and sexual gratification,
—a mechanism of tension reduction,
—a means of legitimate procreation,
—social placement,
—an approach to inter-family alliance and group solidarity, and
—above all, an act of piety.[16]

Both above definitions and purposes are quite elaborate and comprise many views about the functions of the family. Nevertheless, there is the intricate cause and effect relationship between the family and society.

The culture of any society comprises many traditions installed in its individuals' minds and which are passed on from one generation to another. As man is conservative by instinct, he does not try to change such traditions except under the great pressure of evolutionary requirements. This perpetual struggle between the two instincts: conservatism and evolution plays an important role in delimiting the functions of the family institution in every society. Both instincts are dynamic and must be kept in good balance for any sane society to develop. Traditions constitute a part of the established ideology of a people, whilst evolution is the active element that steers the present status towards a future one, and as such, it formulates another part of the ideology. Amidst this continuous process the family exists, caught between the two parts. The family is there to conserve what is best and most appropriate in tradition, and to adopt and practice what is best and most appropriate in the new evolution.

To apply the above philosophy, functions, and definitions to the Muslim family in the States, we come immediately to a host of variegated and intertwined problems. Islam is integral and Muslims are supposed to adopt it in its entirety. *"Believe ye in part of the Scripture and disbelieve ye in part thereof. And what is the reward of those who do so save ignominy in the life of this world, and in the Day of Resurrection they will be consigned to the most grievous doomed"* (2:85)

Accordingly, they are required to apply Islamic laws concerning all matrimonial matters. Yet, being residents in a non-Muslim country which does not follow the Islamic Shariah, they are bound to meet with a complex of contradictory situations. Such complication is exacerbated by the lack of consolidated Muslim communities and the absence of any Islamic order that could help solve their problems.

To start with, there is the problem of the marriage contract. Muslims who intend to live here for a protracted length of time or forever are obliged to register their marriage in accordance with the laws of the state in which they wed. Once this is done, the rights and obligations of both spouses are defined by what these laws stipulate and not by Islamic injunctions. This applies, in fact, to all subsequent familial issues. The husband's financial obligation towards his wife and household, the wife's duties towards her husband and household, and the social code which should be observed by both—all these important issues become subject to local American jurisprudence. In case of divorce, it is again the state laws that adjudge the final separation act irrespective of the Islamic injunctions.

Another important issue that affects the Muslim family in the States is the economic status. In many cases, both spouses are obliged to work and gain more income to make ends meet and to save something as a security for the future. This economic aspect is very common to most American families and is taken for granted by them, with its good and bad effects. It does not constitute a major problem to them as it is consistent with their material civilization and ideology. Westerners have developed a certain philosophy of life in regard to the status of women as a result of their past heritage and present industrialized societies. It is common knowledge that Athenians treated women as a commodity which could be bought and sold. The Romans considered women to be the property of the father and/or the husband until the days of Justinian (5th century) when some separate identity of women was legally acknowledged. Judaism looks down upon women as a curse worse than death and considers them essentially evil. The Christian views on women varied from considering them to be living beings without souls to humans without identity. The British law until 1801 allowed the husband to sell his wife. The list of historical abuses of women in the West is too long to be enumerated in this paper.

It is only very recently that non-Muslim societies agreed to give women some independent status. Even today, the renowned liberal opportunity outside marriage, supported by contraception and abortion."[18]

The main purpose of marriage has become to satiate the desires of the couple, or what the libs call to achieve individual fulfillment and to ascertain the spouse's identity. The new concept has become tantamount to fulfilling the "desire of each other's need for individual happiness" and "the development of man-woman relationship." This, according to them, would lead to giving the wife the same status as the husband without differentiation or discrimination. Thus, a new concept of marriage rooted in the family had to be developed, and four substitutes are being practiced in modern societies:

1. Serial monogamy, where a series of marriages take place one after the other. This is what prevails in the United States at present where divorce occurs in 40% of marriages and where 75% of the divorced remarry. There are some modernists who suggest the "bypass of divorce by requiring renewal or cancellation of all marriage contracts at three year intervals."[19]

2. Open marriage, where the exclusivity of husband-wife (sexually and otherwise) is eliminated. Those who advocate this category of marriage practice "wife swapping" or "swinging." They claim that extramarital experiences would reduce jealousy, relieve tensions and ease the pressures of personal conflict.

3. Polygamy and group marriage where an association of husbands and wives and their children mix together without restriction or constraint. The claim here is that multiplicity of parenthood for adults and children would offer a wider variety of interactive experiences in meeting individual needs.

4. Homosexuality, where women "marry" women and men "marry" men without the usual conflict which is inevitable in every new normal marriage.

All such approaches can never succeed in creating a happy family because they ignore the biological and the spiritual elements. Humans cannot survive without a society and no society can survive without the family. As individuals, "to live is to love and to love is to live," as Havelock Ellis puts it. Serial monogamy, open marriage, group marriage and homosexuality lack the premodial basics of the family. Humans are the only species where the offspring needs parental catering for a rela-

American wife cannot buy property without the consent of her husband nor is she allowed to stick to her maiden name without adding that of her husbands.[17] In Switzerland, she cannot enter into any contractual transaction without her husband's written consent, and if she earns any money from her work, he is legally entitled to half her income. All over the West, the husband can deprive his wife of his legacy after death.

No wonder, then, we hear women claiming "equality" with man and justice in treatment. The present culture, predominantly influenced by the economic or materialistic agent, gave justice, equality and liberation a material implication—a pecuniary value. In their industrial age where money is power, where rich is good and poor is bad, where dog eat dog are accepted premises of individuals' interrelations, and where moral values have been dumped into the garbage bin, women are contending for economic independence as a basis for their claim for equal human rights. To achieve this end, they did not mind the commercialization of their femininity, the loss of their chastity, the destruction of their family and the perturbation of their emotions. This yearning for liberation pushed the Western woman into deep waters. Her desire for independence dragged her into competition and aggression, and her pride alienated her from the affectionate society. In her solitude, she accepted permissiveness and along with her struggle for survival, she nurtured bitterness and rancor. In the midst of her secular preoccupation, she suppressed her spiritual values and trod on her motherly instincts.

The American concept of family and marriage has undergone radical change in the last few decades. Originally, as Edward Westermack puts it, "Marriage is rooted in the family and not the family in marriage." The family in turn was the foundation of society. Hence, the regulation of all family relations was considered a necessity called for by two fundamental exigencies: wholesome human procreation and preservation of society. The modern industrial culture upset the past norm of family life and greatly changed the purposes of marriage. New opportunities of material gain were opened to married and unmarried. Women making them economically independent from their husbands and male providers. The women's emancipation movement accordingly declared that there was no more reason for tolerating subjugation to the male and cultivated the eccentric tendencies against the traditional functioning and sex-roles in the family. "The woman's new freedom has greatly increased sexual

tively long period after birth, not only physically but emotionally as well. The new frustrated efforts, as reflected in the modern abnormal family life do not unite man and woman in a bond where both enjoy material and emotional security, stability and contentment. They do not cure the ailments created by the prevailing technological culture: alienation, loneliness, anomie, lack of love, and anxiety. "Search any average human being and you soon find evidence of heart-hunger for closeness and intimacy and the shared life as the only dependable sources of a sustained sense of self-esteem and of personal worth."[20]

The women's emancipation movement in this country is revolting against long-standing inequitable treatment, against a biased, unjust legal system and a domineering economic exploitation. In their revolt, and in the absence of any effective religious or moral guidance, women have gone to the extreme which has brought down on them the misery of "civilized prostitution and adultery."

Such are the circumstances of the culture under which a Muslim family lives in this country. It would be a gross mistake to assume that Muslims will not be affected by the American way of life, the American materialistic values and American laws. Hence, the complex of problems of Muslim families start. If we add to the above anomalies the problems arising from the educational systems and its repercussions on the youngsters and adults, we could better understand the vast dimension of the Muslim dilemma. An example of this confusion is the so-to-speak highly educated Muslim wife who believes that it is her legitimate right to invite any male friend into the home, even in the absence of her husband, to accept an invitation in another city or another country without his permission, or the right to choose hard work in a locality other than where he lives. It is not a rare case to come across a Muslim woman who believes that she has the right to work as she has spent long years qualifying herself in a certain profession. In most cases, she would be motivated by her desire to material gain, especially when she can have some fulfillment out of the social activities in her professional domain. Such wives are deeply influenced by the American materialistic mentality and would claim the best of two worlds: to keep her job and to claim her Islamic right to be sustained by her husband.

The problems of children born in Muslim families are well known to all and have been repeatedly discussed by Muslim sociologists and thinkers in numerous conventions and symposia. They revolve on the cold fact that the American environment and culture affect the Muslim child's mentality and code of ethical values. When both parents are working, the child does not get enough care and domestic orientation to protect him against anti-Islamic practices. More serious a menace is the loss of the child's Islamic identity and his relatedness to a Muslim community. But these children's problems are mainly derived from the principal family problems which, if solved, would automatically bring relief to the children's ordeal.

THE ISLAMIC SOLUTION
BIOLOGY AND SOCIALIZATION

There is nothing more compatible with human nature than Islamic teachings and injunctions, if only because they take the individual as a fallible being, subject to trial and error and subject to correction and evolution. *"On no soul does God place a burden greater than it can bear"* (2:286)

It gets every good that it earns, and it suffers every ill that it earns. As we are concerned here with the Muslim family, it is natural that whatever solution we may suggest, it must be in accordance with Islam. Luckily enough, Islam decides upon every issue, taking human nature in consideration and exhorting us to abide by the eternal laws of creation. Empirical sciences have discovered many facts concerning our biological structure and physiological functioning, but there are still many more of life's secrets to be uncovered. There is not one single established scientific fact that runs contrary to any Islamic injunction; but there are many postulates, ideas and theories that may be incompatible with Islamic teachings. Under such uncertain conditions, the Muslim is supposed to follow the Islamic rules irrespective of the scientific dubious points of view and his personal desires.

Regarding the traditions and cultures that affect our socialization, we must bear in mind that these are the product of certain practiced ideals and established ideas prevailing at one time in a certain society. This is an extremely important element in the Islamic syndrome of solutions to societal problems. Islam is a philosophy that defines the purpose of human life, the relation between man, nature, and the Creator. It is a doctrine that sets up the broad outlines of the social, political, economic and esthetic systems which should be applied in our daily transactions and intercourse. Such philosophical definitions and doctrinal delineations are confined to the basic facts which do not evolve or change in accordance with the continuous human evolution. Facts are absolute and are not subject to change, otherwise they are neither facts nor absolute.

Whatever solutions we find in Islam, they are based on such absolute facts whether known to our contemporary scientists or unknown to them. The entire concept of the family and roles of its members is a part of the general concept of the Islamic society. Let us bear in mind that marriage is dictated by our biological needs and is a part of the indispensable human society and not just a matter of individual option. *"And of everything we have created pairs"* (51:49).

The word '*zawj*' is used in the Quran as meaning a pair or a mate. Both words connote marriage. *"Do they not look at the earth, how many pairs of noble things we have produced therein"* (31:10). Even in Paradise, the Quran informs us that we shall have mates (see 2:25, 4:57). God created humans from one soul, which could be the first cell. From this soul He created the male and the female. The story of creating Eve (the first female) from a rib of Adam (the first male) is not mentioned in the Quran. *"And among His signs is this, that He created for you mates from yourselves that ye may find rest (and peace) in them"* (30:21). *"'O mankind, heed (in reverence) your Lord Who created you from a single soul and from it created its mate and from them twain both spread multitude of men and women"* (4:1).

Our Prophet orders us to get married as soon as we can. The family is the nucleus of the Islamic society and marriage is the only way to bring about such an institution. Extra-marital relations are categorically condemned and prohibited. *"Nor come nigh to adultery (or fornication) for it is a shameful deed and an evil, opening the road to other evils"* (17:30).

It is only logical that Islam set up the rules to regulate the functioning of the family whereby both spouses can find peace, love, security and relatedness. The elements are necessary to accomplish the greatest purpose of marriage: the worship of God. By worship it is not only meant the performance of rituals, but it essentially implies righteousness in all transactional behavior. Every good deed, every service to humanity, every useful productive effort, and even every good word are a part of a true

Muslim worship of his God. If both husband and wife observe this main purpose, this cardinal purpose of their union, they would easily learn how to help each other achieve this goal which is greater than themselves. They would learn how to tolerate each other, how to love God in themselves and in other beings, and how to overcome their difficulties and their shortcomings.

The second purpose of marriage is to respond to the basic biological instinct of procreation. Children are the realization of motherhood and fatherhood. Islam is particular in providing the most possible wholesome atmosphere for bringing up the offspring. To give birth to children and neglect them is a crime towards society, the children, and the parents themselves. The child who is deprived of the ample love of his or her parents, who is not properly tutored at an early age, and who is left to babysitters and nurseries will develop many anti-social behavioral patterns and may end up with crime, perversion and corruption. Such a child may never find his or her identity as he or she could have felt it in a systematic manner during his or her childhood. Without a family life, governed by Islamic order and discipline, how can we expect a child to have the Muslim conscience and the Islamic value of righteousness.

Islam prescribes clear rights and obligations on parents and their descendent Parents are legally responsible for the education and maintenance of their children. These, by turn, are legally responsible for accommodating and maintaining their parents, if they so require, in their old age. Both parents and children inherit from each other according to a prescribed and accurate law of inheritance specified in the Quran. Neither of them can deprive the other of their respective shares in the legacy. This is only part of the long family code in Islam. What is of import here is the husband-wife relationship—their sex roles—within the context of Islamic comprehension: "*And among His Signs is this, that He created for you mates from among yourselves, that you may find rest (and peace) in them. And He has put love and mercy between your (hearts); Verily in this are signs for those who reflect*" (30:21).

Despite the importance of these moral values: rest, peace, love and mercy, Islam did not stop there. It bolstered its original concept of the family by defining the roles of man and woman in such a manner that each should act in accordance with his or her biological merits. The man, with his aggression, is charged with what is called the instrumental functions: maintenance, protection, dealings with the outworldly matters and leadership within the family. The woman is entrusted with caring for and rearing the children, organizing the home, and creating the loving atmosphere inside. Let us be clear from the beginning that in an Islamic society the wife is not expected to be pushed to work to gain money. Even the unmarried, the divorcee, and the widow are guaranteed, by law, an income that helps them lead a reasonably comfortable life. Work or trade are not prohibited to women. Yet, they are not recommended to undertake such activities unless there is a justification for them and without prejudice to their husband's rights. Once the woman gets married, she accepts the Islamic ruling on the functioning of the family. Her role becomes mainly to achieve the welfare of her household and to look after the internal family affairs. If she wants to work, she is bound to ask the explicit approval of her husband. However, if she has her own property or fortune, and if she opts to run or invest such wealth, she is entitled to do so without her husband's permission, but provided this does not infringe upon her marital obligations.

THE ISLAMIC FAMILY

In Islam, as in biology, there is no family without marriage, and there is no marriage without rules and discipline. The family in Islam is a unit in which two independent persons unite and share life together. The husband's dignity is an integral part of his wife's dignity. Accordingly, neither of them is better than the other. To unite and share, there must be mutual love and compassion—a genuine feeling which unless translated into action and behavior would be mere illusion and futile emotion. One can hardly accept the claim of love of the spouse who does not care for his or her sick partner or who does not share the family responsibilities. This fundamental basis, if well understood and observed, makes the first loyalty of both spouses to their family which is supposed to serve God in piety as the main purpose of marriage. It implies that they act as if they were one person with many organs. The head of the human is not better than the heart, and the hand is not better than the foot. If the man is charged with the duty of leadership and maintenance, he is not better than the woman who is assigned the duty of keeping the household, even if the first duty is more difficult and perhaps more significant. Imam

Muhammad Abduh emphasizes this point as vital for the right under-standing of the sex roles of spouses. He adds that the Quranic verse, *"And in no wise covet those things in which God hath bestowed His gifts more freely on some of you than on others: to men is allotted what they earn, and to women what they earn,"* (4:32) does not imply that every man is better than every woman or vice versa. According to him, each sex, in general, has some preferential advantage over the other, though men have a degree over women.[21]

There has been much controversy about this 'degree'. Some interpret it as the delegation of leadership, surveillance and maintenance which are bestowed on men. Others say that it is the tolerance with which men must treat their wives. A third view is that it is men's natural gift for judging matters and managing external problems. However, the consensus is that this 'degree' comprises the principle of 'guardianship' or *'qiwamah'*.

Imam Abduh in the course of interpreting the preceding Quranic verse, stated that *qiwamah* or guardianship has four elements: protection, surveillance, custody and maintenance. Dr. Abd al-Ati considered the ele-ment of obedience over and above the aforementioned four elements— the most important indication of *qiwamah*. Obedience, to him, and in accordance to the Quran and Traditions comprises the following:

1. She must not receive male, strangers or accept gifts from them without his permission. Nor must she lend or dispose of any of his pos-sessions without his approval.

2. The husband has the legal right to restrict her freedom of move-ment and prevent her from leaving her home without his permission. She must comply with this right unless there is a necessity or legitimate advantage for her to do otherwise. However, it is his religious obligation to be compassionate so as to relax his right to restrict her freedom of movement. If there arises a conflict between this right of his and wife's parents' right to visit and be visited by their daughter, his right prevails. Yet it is religiously recommended that he be considerate enough to waive his right and avoid estrangement within his conjugal family or between any member of this family and close relatives, e.g. the wife's parents.

3. A refractory wife has no legal right to object to the husband's exer-cise of his disciplining authority. Islamic law, in common with most other systems of law, recognizes the husband's right to discipline his wife for disobedience.

4. The wife may not legally object to the husband's right to take another wife or to exercise his right of divorce. The marital contract establishes her implicit consent to these rights. However, if she wishes to restrict his freedom in this regard or to have similar rights, she is legally allowed to do so. She may stipulate in the marital agreement that she too, will have the right to divorce, or that she will keep the marriage bond only so long as she remains the only wife; should he take a second wife, the first will have the right to seek a divorce in accordance with the marriage agreement.

5. Finally, if the husband insists on patrilocality or neolocality, the wife must comply."[22]

CONCLUSION

The problems facing Muslim families living in the States can be dealt with in compliance with Islamic teachings and principles once we accept them as binding. If the spouses are really devout, they will have no difficulty in encountering the evils of the Western culture and in escaping the anti-Islamic societal factors that may run contrary to Islam. The guidelines as we see them would be:

1. The main purpose of marriage is to live in piety and to serve the Islamic Cause. The wife has the right to discontinue working whenever she pleases. The husband may allow the wife to work with the condition that her gain belongs to the family and not be considered as her personal property.

2. Household: When the wife is not employed, the household becomes her first occupation. By household it is meant the rearing of the children and all domestic services required for maintaining a clean and comfortable habitation. The Prophet (ﷺ) said, "Cleanliness is a part of faith." Motherhood is highly appraised in Islam and is the most elated value second to the worship of God.

MARRIAGE, DISPUTES AND DIVORCE

Marriage: Muslims should marry according to Islamic traditions and rules. The marriage will have to be registered with the State in which they wed in order to give it a legal force. This legal procedure subjects the marriage contract to the jurisdiction of American laws which, in most cases, contradict many Islamic rulings. However, such contradiction does not happen unless there is a dispute that both spouses fail to solve in accordance with the *Shariah*.

Disputes: These are expected to arise in all matrimonial relations. Muslim abiding spouses must learn how to compromise and tolerate each other. Their guide is the teaching of their religion and their good example is their Prophet.

However, in case they fail to solve their own problems, they have to resort to arbitration. The spouse who refuses this Quranic injunction or who defies the other partner taking shelter under the umbrella of American laws is failing in his or her religious commitment. The Quranic arbitration is meant to be binding on both spouses and would, indeed, relieve the Muslim family of most of its problems.

Divorce: If one to the spouses refuses arbitration, non-Islamic divorce is bound to take place, leaving a deep painful scar on both of them. Arbitration may end in divorce, but in this case it would be least harmful as both would feel more content when *Shariah* is justly applied.

It is a pity that many recalcitrant (*nashiz*). Muslim women think that American law would serve their interest more than the Islamic Law. This is not only wrong but the consequences of litigation generally leaves more ill feeling than should be.

ENVIRONMENT AND CHILDREN

Nobody can deny the impact of environment upon adults and children. Up until now, one can safely say that Muslims of America could not constitute any physical or moral community comparable to that of the Jews or the Chinese. Granted that there are some groupings in scattered localities and spiritual guidance from different sources, yet there is no community that could respond to many basic needs. The family must live in a society, and unless an Islamic community is created, the Muslim family will have no alternative but to merge in a non-Muslim one.

The danger is so imminent that it forms the major part of the family problems in the United States. Both adults and children are influenced by American values and traditions, and by American behavior and manners. There is no escape from this "assimilation" except by strengthening the family bonds and by steadfast observation of Islamic teachings. The husband must lead here by strict adherence to Islamic ways of life and by requiring the same from his wife.

Such are the sex-roles in Islam and the main problems facing Muslim families in the United States and, indeed, in all non-Muslim countries. The solutions mentioned above entirely depend upon the faith of the spouses and their earnest desire to live up to their religion. God, according to the Holy Quran, has made men in charge of their wives, has ordered them to maintain and protect them and has ordered women to obey their husbands and guard their secrets (see 4:34, 35). As for those spouses who claim the right to twist the meanings of Quranic texts so as to suit their personal desires, and those who try to subject Islam to non-Islamic laws are sick in their hearts and are transgressors. Most probably, such persons would not like to read this essay, though we pray to Allah to guide them to the right way: "*Say: This is my Way: I call on God with sure knowledge and whosoever follows me—glory be to God—and I am not of the idolaters*" (12:108).

NOTES

1. L. Cadmure and L. Larson, "The Center of Life," The New York Times Book Co., 1977, p. 8.

2. *Ibid.*, p. 9.

3. *Ibid.*, p. 28.

4. *Ibid.*, p. 38.

5. I. R. Symthies, "Brain Mechanisms and Behavior." New York: Academic Press, 1970, p. 156.

6. Shirley Weitz, "Sex Roles." New York: Oxford University Press, 1977, p. 7.

7. K. E. Moyer, "Sex Difference in Aggression." Quoted in R. C. Friedman, R. M. Richart, R. L. Vande Wiele, eds., "Sex Differences in Behavior," Wile, 1974, p. 156.

8. Weitz, *op. cit.*, p. 42.

9. D. B. Lynn, "The Father: His Role in Child Development," Monterey, CA: Brooks Cole, 1974, pp. 14-21.

10. Weitz, *op. cit.*, p. 42.

11. M. A. Diamond, "A Critical Evaluation of the Ontogeny of Human Sexual Behavior," Quarterly Review of Biology, 50 (1965), pp. 147-175.

12. Weitz, *op. cit.*, p. 5.

13. Cadmure, *op. cit.*, p. 8.

14. *Ibid.*, p. 39.

15. Hammudah Abd al-Ati, "The Family Structure in Islam." Indiana: American Trust Publications, 1977, p. 19.

16. *Ibid.*, pp. 54-55.

17. Lately a few states have allowed married women to use their maiden names.

18. R. H. Williams (ed). *To Live and To Die*. "Marriage: Whence and Whither," NY: Springer-Verlad, 1973, p. 298.

19. *Ibid.*, p. 299.

20. *Ibid.*, p. 304.

21. *Tafsir al-Manar*, vol. 5, p. 68 ff.

22. Abd al-Ati, *op. cit.*, pp. 172-173. These rights and obligations are corroborated by the Quran and Hadith.

5

GENDER RELATIONS ATTITUDE SURVEY OF MUSLIM YOUTH AND PARENTS

SHAHID ATHAR

I f we as parents do not teach our children about sex, they will probably gain information from the wrong source. Teaching sex education in mixed classes to hot-blooded teenagers without benefit of moral values is like pouring gasoline on emotional fires."

Tim LaHaye
Family Life Services
Author of several books on
sex and marriage

During a presentation at the Islamic Center in Toledo, Ohio, a survey of sex attitude was obtained. A total of 157 attendees out of 200 responded. 95 were parents and 62 were youth. Toledo's Muslim community is well established, educated and progressive and has a mixture of Arab and Indo-Pakistani immigrants. To each question, their (parent vs. youth) response is given.

1. Should an Islamic viewpoint on sexuality be presented in the Weekend Islamic School?

Parents		Youth
Yes:	88 (92%)	52 (83%)
No:	7 (8%)	10 (17%)

2. Should parents teach sex education at home?

Yes:	82 (86%)	47 (75%)
No:	13 (14%)	15 (25%)

3. Are you aware that sex education classes in public schools do not teach moral views and abstinence?

Yes:	72 (75%)	46 (74%)
No:	23 (25%)	16 (26%)

4. Do you allow social mixing of boys and girls above 12 years of age?

Yes	64 (67%)	32 (51%)
No	31 (33%)	30 (49%)

5. Should parents supervise such activities when they are permitted?

Yes	94 (99%)	48 (77%)
No	1 (1%)	14 (23%)

6. Should parents be aware of and choose the movies, TV shows, music and magazines children are exposed to?

Yes	93 (98%)	45 (72%)
No	2 (2%)	17 (28%)

INTERPRETATION OF THE DATA

It is obvious from this survey that both parents and youth as a majority approve of sex education being given at home or at Sunday Islamic School. Nearly two-thirds of them approve of supervised mixing of boys and girls. While the majority of parents feel that they should choose movies, music, TV programs for their youth, the youths themselves, who otherwise are conservative, are equally divided on this issue. We hope that with continued emphasis on Islamic perspective on sex education that their attitude may change in the future.

6

SEX EDUCATION QUESTIONS FROM MUSLIM YOUTH

SHAHID ATHAR

After my presentation on sex education guidelines for Muslim youth and parents at the Islamic Center in Toledo, Ohio, in 1992, many questions were asked by Muslim youth. The Toledo Muslim community is progressive, affluent and has an even mixture of Arab and Indo-Pakistani immigrants.

I compiled all the written questions submitted to me, answered them to the best of my knowledge, and then sent the questions to the late Dr. Mahmood Abu Saud, the well-known scholar, for a second opinion. He did not know my answers. Some of the answers have already been published in the *Islamic Monitor*, the magazine of the Islamic Society of Toledo, in English and Arabic.

After each question, Dr. Abu Saud's reply and my reply are given for comparison.

1. Please explain the importance of *hijab*: What is the degree of sin if mature Muslim sister does not wear a dress properly (cover her head, etc.)?

Abu Saud: The word *"hijab"* is used in the Holy Quran in its linguistic original sense, i.e., a barrier, something to separate two things from one another. The Prophet's wives were ordered by God to observe *hijab*, meaning not to face all mature males who are entitled to marry them. They had to speak to such males from behind a curtain or a door so nobody would see them.

In our times, the word is usually used to indicate the dress of a woman in accordance with the Islamic requirements. What is definite for man and woman is that neither gender should dress or act in a way that is intended to attract the attention of the opposite sex. By instinct, males are more attracted to females' bodies than vice versa. Accordingly, Islam ordained that women should not show of their bodies what would particularly attract the attention of males. Besides, they should not show of their adornment other than that conventionally shown by women in an Islamic society.

As for the degree of sin, it depends upon the degree of violating these rules and the intention of the female who violates them. There are no fast rules determining the details of how to dress and cover other than to be modest and not show off.

Athar: *hijab* is an injunction from God (33:59). The extent of *hijab* can be questioned. However, obeying/disobeying an injunction altogether is a reflection of the faith of the person. The degree of sin or forgiving is up to the Law Maker.

2. When one is engaged, are you allowed to go out with your fiancee?

Abu Saud: Yes, provided there is no touching, necking and no staying behind closed doors or in a place where they would not be seen by others. Engagement in Islam is not a contract of marriage binding on either party .

Athar: No, not alone, unless a third adult member of the family is present, i.e., brother, sister or one of the parents.

3. Can a Muslim marry someone his parents disapprove of?

Abu Saud: Yes, as long as the marrying person is legally entitled to marriage.

Athar: Yes, however, one must find out why the parent(s) object to this marriage, as maybe they are right. Is the person you plan to marry an alcoholic, a drug dealer, a pimp? This is not a question of your or your parents' right but a question of your communications with your parents.

4. What are your views on Muslim teens (boys/girls) talking socially?

Abu Saud: It is healthy for boys and girls to talk and socialize as long as they do that within the Islamic moral code: no obscenity, no touching, no secret appointments, etc. They should talk socially in order to know each other as ordained by God in Quran (*Surah al-Hujrat*). However, one must be careful about what this social talking leads to.

Athar: They should talk socially in order to know each other as ordained by God in the Quran (*Surah al-Hujrat*). However, one must be careful in what this social talking leads to.

5. If you think abortion is murder, then what would happen if it were illegal? Ladies would do it at home, punch themselves in the stomach, and then they and the babies would die.

Abu Saud: Most of the Muslim jurists do not think that abortion before the end of the third month is murder, although they declare it reprehensible unless there is a legitimate justification. If it is illegal, then it is the woman's problem; she should have taken enough precaution not to get pregnant.

Athar: A crime is a crime, no matter how noble your intention is and means to achieve it. In this case both fetus and mother may die (a double crime).

6. According to statistics, the majority of teenagers who do not even have orgasm when they have sex. The orgasm they get is when they talk about it in the locker room.

Abu Saud: If so, why have sex? Orgasm is the acme of sexual pleasure. However, talking about it simply arouses the instinct and does not help in sublimating the desire. Granted, girls and boys cannot avoid thinking of it, but it would be more healthy to talk about it in the open with a responsible person, although in such cases, most probably there will be no orgasm.

Athar: Not true! Orgasm is related to duration and extent of foreplay and not intensity of sex. In the locker room, they can pretend they have orgasm to impress others.

7. How does one go about finding a suitable practicing Muslim spouse?

Abu Saud: Islamically speaking, both boys and girls are entitled to propose to the other sex. Thus, frequent gatherings of Muslims allow you to talk to whomever you feel like being your mate, one or more, take their addresses and write to them, invite them into your house and keep your parents informed of what you are doing. Attend youth conferences. Try to participate in discussions and lectures so as to expose yourself and become noticeable. You may also publish an advertisement in *Islamic Horizon.*

Athar: Stay in the community of practicing Muslims, doing things in the community in which you are known, and let your friends and family know that you are ready and available. Once you find one, let him/her know indirectly that you like him/her, preferably through your parents.

8. You are giving the wrong idea to the parents. You are making them think when girls and boys are friends, it is bad. . .WHY?

Abu Saud: When boys and girls work together for doing good, they become friends. When they meet in public such as in conferences, youth camps and in study rooms and the like, they become friends. When boys and girls start meeting in hiding, or in secrecy without informing their guardians, when they start to touch each other's bodies, when they start a love affair, even without sleeping together, this is not an innocent friendship, and should he discouraged.

Athar: I did not give this idea. See answer #4.

9. You talk about monogamy. Our society in the Muslim world is not monogamous but polygamous. They are allowed to have four wives. Those are their right to possess as well as slaves.

Abu Saud: There is no question to answer, but the above statement is a wrong point of view. Polygamy is not common in the Muslim world, although it exists. There are strict terms set in the Quran on marrying more than one woman, and they are really difficult to observe. However, a woman can always indicate in her marriage contract that she would not accept to be with another wife, and can even insist on an important compensation in case she is divorced for no fault of her own. Whatever the case may be, to have another wife is much better than to have a mistress. If in the inquirer's view, polygamy is slavery, the second wife should not accept it.

Athar: Muslim society in the Muslim world is by practice monogamous. There is less than one percent polygamy, and that is by permission and not injunction. In the West, men who can control their desire, have one wife and one to four mistresses. Also in the West, they practice polygamy but not at the same time, i.e., cycle of marriage, divorce, marriage and divorce several times in their lives.

10. Is there any harm in men and women sitting together, in this lecture hall for instance. It seems natural that a family sit together with other family and friends. We seem to do this everywhere except here.

Abu Saud: There is no harm in men and women sitting together. They used to do so in the days of the Prophet, and the books of *hadith* are full of such instances. You are right in your observation, and it is for you and others of some moral courage and clean thoughts to stand up and DO JUST THAT: SIT TOGETHER.

Athar: Islam believes in separation of sexes in social gatherings unless people are *mahram* to each other (see *Surah Ahzab* and *Surah Nur*). This is natural, even in secular schools, that girls like to sit, walk or play with girls rather than boys. Unnecessary social mixing may lead to other wrongs. The Creator of the human body knows what is good for us and we don't.

11. What should a Muslim boy do if he is constantly rejected when he proposes?

Abu Saud: He must be following the wrong approach and procedure, or there must be something basically wrong with him. Counseling would be very useful in this case.

Athar: He should find out why he/she is being rejected. Maybe it is the way he/she proposed, etc.

12. What is the Islamic rule concerning masturbation?

Abu Saud: There is no authentic text prohibiting masturbation, although it is reprehensible on account of two man factors: It leads to sexual arousal and more desire, and it actually affects the health, especially for boys. Sex is like any other natural instinct in that the more you think of it, the more it is accentuated. Generally speaking, humans sublimate and administer their instincts. We want to possess, but we work and earn; we want to eat, but we control our eating habits; and we want to have sex, but we marry.

Athar: Masturbation is considered *makruh* (detestable) in Islam; i.e., it is between lawful and permitted. Some scholars of the past have permitted it to students and soldiers who are single in a non-Muslim society where temptation is high, in order to save them from adultery. The medical harms are not confirmed.

13. If you are an unmarried Muslim girl and pregnant, what choices do you have: Abortion, adoption, etc.?

Abu Saud: The first option is to marry the father of the child. The second is to have an abortion in the first three months of pregnancy. The third is to keep the child, and the fourth is to give him/her up for adoption providing the child keeps his father's name.

Athar: Abortion if the health of the mother is physically or mentally threatened; otherwise, carry to term, then adoption or even marriage with the boy if possible. Hopefully, Muslim girls don't come to this difficult stage and marry beforehand. If they are ready for sex, they should be ready for marriage.

14. In what circumstances are abortions allowed and are we Muslims allowed to use contraceptives?

Abu Saud: About abortion, see question #6. About contraceptives, they are allowed in Islam by explicit statement of the Prophet (ﷺ) where he did not forbid *coitus interruptis.*

Athar: Abortions are not allowed unless it is a matter of rape and incest, and the health of the mother is concerned. Chemical contraceptives, i. e ., birth control for married women, is allowed though not promoted because of its many medical side effects.

15. What is the right age to get married in this society?

Abu Saud: There is no fast rule fixing such an age. When a person is mature enough, can live independently and is ready to meet the responsibilities of marriage, he/she can marry.

Athar: In this society, about a million girls get pregnant each year, and if they were married, they would not be counted in teenage pregnancy statistics. This right age is when you are ready to marry. If you have achieved puberty, then you must abstain from sex until you think you are ready for marriage. Otherwise, you may fall into the sin of premarital sex.

16. How does one go about proposing to either a boy or a girl?

Abu Saud: If you know the person, simply talk about your desire to get married and wait for the reaction. Then, if the reaction is positive, just express your desire to engage the person. If the answer is positive again, inform both families and arrange for the "official" engagement.

Athar: You let him/her know your intention to marry him/her, through your parents or trusted friends.

17. I see a lot of women in this hall without *hijab*. We know this is against Islam and against the Prophet's teaching. I would like to know why.

Abu Saud: The answer depends on what you do mean by *hijab* (see question #1). If it is only uncovering of hair while the body is well covered, then the question is controversial. Slave women during the days of the Prophet even used to pray without covering their hair. Men never were seen uncovering their hair in public, but that was a societal convention. The idea of covering hair is the same as covering the adornment and the body of the woman. In simple words, as women are very proud of their hair and do consider it a part of their beauty that attracts the attention of men, it is then supposed to be covered.

Athar: See answer #1.

18. All religions prohibit premarital sex and consider that as sin. Why don't all religious leaders put their point across to the government and not leave this subject to the big "L" liberals?

Abu Saud: Because sex in the society in which we live is liberal; and accordingly, the government elected by the people is liberal.

Athar: Government does not control personal expressions or emotions. The good and bad, and right and wrong have to be recognized and accepted individually.

19. Is abortion allowed if the life of the woman is in danger and/or you have amniocentesis and find the child could be handicapped/ Down's syndrome?

Abu Saud: If there is danger for the mother, abortion would be allowed. If there will definitely be a congenital defect, then the matter depends on the degree of this defect. If it is so serious that the child will not be able to function at all, or will not be able to live on his own, then the question is controversial. In all cases, if abortion takes place in the first three months (that is, four months from the last period), it may be carried out.

Athar: Yes, under medical decision.

20. What if you want a child but don't want to get married?

Abu Saud: Adopt a child according to the Islamic rules: Mainly, keep the child's father's name and no inheritance. He will never be YOUR child.

Athar: You will have to have another man's sperm, which is adultery. When the child is born, he/she would like to know the father. What will you tell him/her that will satisfy and make him/her happy?

21. Is there anything wrong with being married young?

Abu Saud: No, as long as you are ready for marriage. See question #15. The Prophet (ﷺ) says, "He who can afford to get married, let him marry. . . "

Athar: No, unless you are marrying a man who is too old.

22. What is sex?

Abu Saud: Sex is the cohabitation of a male with a female for the purpose of reproduction. A married couple may decide not to have children and still they legitimately perform sex. Sex without marriage is illegitimate and is obviously harmful to the individuals and their society.

Athar: Sex is the act of intimacy between two people of the opposite or same sex, starting with being together, to foreplay and the sexual act. The best sex organ is said to be the brain; other organs are hand and mouth.

23. Why are Muslim men allowed to marry non-Muslim women and Muslim women not allowed to marry non-Muslim men?

Abu Saud: The Quran says, *"Do not marry (your girls) to unbelievers until they believe"* (2:221). The family structure is so paternal that the n on-Muslim father would dominate and dictate. This meant that the children would be non-Muslims, that the wife would not be free to practice her religion, and that the different laws of Islam (such as inheritance, alimony, guardianship, etc.) cannot be observed. Accordingly, such marriage would lead to what is prohibited and thus becomes prohibited.

Athar: Not true. Muslim men are allowed to marry women from only people of book (Jews and Christians), not Hindu or atheist, etc. Even then they are encouraged to prefer believing women even if she is a slave than idolater. The reason Muslim women are not allowed non-Muslim men are many to include the future of children.

24. Are Muslim girls allowed to play sports?

Abu Saud: Yes, of course. In public, she must be covered, and if she plays with boys, there should be no touching.

Athar: Yes, only with girls.

25. Islam is a very patriarchal and sexist religion. Why is the podium faced toward the men? Why don't you direct your speech toward the women? A woman will look attractive to a man, and that is why she must cover up, right? Well, have you ever thought that maybe a woman will also find a man attractive? Why should not he cover up? Why are men placed on a higher stool than women? Is that really what God wants?

Abu Saud: Islam is not patriarchal or sexist; it is YOUR society which is both. The Prophet (ﷺ) used to talk to women directly, facing them. He, and the caliphs after him, used to address them, answer their questions and sell to and buy from them. Both men and women are required to cast down their eyesight and be modest. By instincts men are more attracted to the woman's body than vice versa, and that is why she must cover up. However, man, being obligated to earn the living of the family and to protect it, has to work and mix with others, such that covering up would not be practical.

Athar: Not true, as men and women in the audience could hear the speaker the same way.

26. What is the right age to get married in this society? Can you marry a person whom your parents do not approve of?

Abu Saud: See question #3 and question #15.

Athar: See question #3. The right age is when a person is physically and emotionally mature and ready for marriage. In this society, more than a million teenage girls become pregnant each year. If they are ready for sex, they should be ready for sex with responsibility and commitment which comes from marriage.

27. Right of inheritance to a fetus: the rape situation in Islamic countries where rape is monumental and CANNOT be proved.

Abu Saud: The embryo is a prospective inheritor; i.e., if the father dies during the pregnancy of his wife, the estate inheritance division will be suspended until the birth or miscarriage of the fetus.

There is no evidence that rape in Muslim countries is monumental, nor is it a fact that proving it is impossible. However, if the father is not known, there would be no inheritance except from the mother.

Athar: In the U.S.A., 200,000 women are raped every year, nearly two per minute, but half of the rapes are not reported. The reporting of rape in Muslim countries is related to weakness within women, for shame or whatever else.

28. Is placing of the private parts to the mouth harmful, for boys and girls alike?

Abu Saud: Oral sex is not forbidden in Islam as long as it is practiced between husband and wife.

Athar: No, but only with your spouse. *"Your women are your tilth for you, so go to your tilth as ye wish"* (2:223). Thus, all sexual positions except anal intercourse are permitted between husband and wives. There may be some medical harm in oral sex if organs are not clean or have infection. In that case they should seek medical treatment first before engaging in sex.

29. Are Muslim boys allowed to wear earrings, or is it a woman's dress?

Abu Saud: The general rule is that men should not try to look like woman and vice versa. If conventionally agreed and accepted, earrings are used only for women; then a Muslim boy should not wear them.

Athar: Men are not allowed to mimic women in dress or other ways including jewelry.

30. Are girls or boys allowed to talk about the opposite sex in a way that conveys a feeling?

Abu Saud: It is human to have feelings towards the other sex. But to talk about it is another matter that depends entirely on what sort of talk it is. Modesty is the key word in this context. One must be decent and modest. One must be clean in thought and deed. God knows what is in the hearts of His servants and the servants must be aware of His cognition.

Athar: Yes, but be cautious not to give the wrong emotion. To play with someone's emotions is not right.

31. Are women allowed to work, leaving their children at home?

Abu Saud: There is no prohibition for women to work. If they have children, it is the responsibility of both parents to look after them. However, it is biologically the mother who should cater to the needs of the child in his early age. Whether she can leave him at home during her working hours or not, is a matter of circumstances and age of the child. What is essential is consideration of the interest of the child as the first priority.

Athar: Not a good idea. This deprives children of her mother's love and presence, both of which are badly needed.

32. What are the Islamic jurisdictions toward marriage?

Abu Saud: In Islam, marriage is a civil (though divine) contract, witnessed first by God, then by the society. The main terms of an Islamic marriage are: the free consent of both spouses, the public declaration of marriage, the dower to the wife, the respect of the terms that either party may opt to include in the contract (such as the wife's condition to be the sole wife, to divorce herself without the consent of the husband without mentioning any reason, or to get her dower at any certain time, etc.), and that the information in the contract is correct (for instance, whether or not either spouse is married, whether or not either of them has a disease, etc.)

Athar: Marriage is ordained by God and is a tradition of Prophet

Muhammad. He said marriage is half of faith and that it is a shield against wrongdoing.

FINAL REMARKS

It is not necessary for the youth or parents who have read the above answers to agree with either mine or those of Dr. Abu Saud, as sometimes we did not agree with each other, either. It is also possible that both of us may be wrong. The purpose of this particular article is to make parents aware of youth's questions and stimulate discussion within a family. Muslim youth, instead of taking our answers for granted, should seek more explanation from their parents, Sunday school teachers, Imam of the mosque and above all, from the Quran and Sunnah. *"It is not befitting a believing man or a believing woman that when God and His Messenger have decided an affair for them, they should after that claim have any say in their affairs and whosoever is rebellious to God and His messenger, he verily goes astray in error manifest"* (33:36).

7
CANDID TALK
Farhad Khan

How do the attitudes of Muslim youth toward sex differ from those of other Americans? How does Islam equip them to deal with the pressures of a promiscuous society, where nearly all their peers are sexually active?

If you are a parent, put aside for a short time your preconceptions of how you think your children feel about their sexual identity and responsibilities. If you are a teenager or college student, much of what will be said here will reflect the experiences of you and your friends because it reflects the reality of the situations that face us all.

Unfortunately, there is no such thing as a perfect society. There will always be those who indulge in social taboos. The reality is that casual, premarital sex happens, and to ignore it will only make the problem worse. This reality becomes:

What do American Muslim youth think about sex? Youth should be taught that it's okay to feel uncomfortable about sex. It's your body's way of telling you that it's not right for you at that time. If Islam is really important to you and you really believe that it prescribes what is best for you in the long run, no amount of pressure should be applied in the society where American Muslim youth are raised since the media blitz on sexuality adds to the already present anxiety and distorts people's views on what is considered right and wrong behavior.

In Islam, sex is more than just a means of procreation. It has a very specific role within the context of marriage, a concept that differs from some religions in that it is integral to the process of pleasing one's partner and creating a loving, nurturing relationship. As children get older and more able to mentally handle the subject, sex should be taught to be the beautiful able to convince you. Sex, in most cases, is an act that is between two people observed by God, and if one of those three is not comfortable with it, then something is wrong. The reality is that it happens, for non-Muslims and Muslims alike, and not talking about it or discussing it and its consequences can only make the problem worse thing that it is, within the context of marriage, so that once they grow up, they will be able to appreciate it for its inherent beauty and purpose.

WHAT ARE THE PRESSURES YOUTH FACE TODAY?

The topic of sexuality provokes strong emotions in people, and because of this reaction, we see sexual images and actions everywhere. Fear, mystery, curiosity, desire—all of these very powerful emotions can be easily manipulated by—and into sexual behavior. "A lot of underage people drink because its frowned upon by authority figures and the same goes for sexual activity," said one teenage Muslim boy. "Basically, a lot of people become curious about sex because of a combination of their peers telling them that they are weird if they don't and their parents telling them they will go to hell if they do." Sexuality is such a complex subject that to dismiss or trivialize it is to suppress a natural urge which demands attention, either through discussion or—as is often the case—release.

"My parents go so far as to tell me what I'm feeling is unnatural, and that I'm being wrong just thinking about the opposite sex in that way," one person said. "I mean, I don't plan to act out on what I'm feeling, but I have to at least talk about it—but not to my parents, I guess." Many young people complain that their parents set unrealistic expectations regarding sexual pressure or anxiety, and they also feel abandoned by parents who simply tell them to "just say no." This leaves them with no choice but to consult less reliable sources of information, such as their equally confused peers.

ISLAM GIVES THE TOOLS TO JUDGE

A healthy background of Islamic ideals can counteract the pressures people face about sex. Nearly all the people interviewed for this article cited Islamic belief as being essential in removing much of the anxiety which plagues American youth. "Islam puts sex into perspective," one youth said. "Unlike some other religions, it's treated as a normal, natural activity that, given a proper context, can bring pleasure and happiness. It isn't necessarily considered 'dirty'—just something worth waiting for."

Most youth agree that education is important. "A lot of our curiosity about sex and sexuality could be satisfied with frank and open discussion," said one. Another said that it is "the mystique surrounding sex in a Muslim family that sparks curiosity. The lure becomes stronger the less your parents discuss it." One parent added that discussing the benefits of sex, like better physical and emotional health, rather than instilling an unnatural fear, is very important. "After all, nobody would bungee jump if it weren't dangerous."

THE RISKS OF SEPARATION

Most Muslim youth, like other Americans, can unfortunately find themselves increasingly susceptible to sexually transmitted diseases and unwanted pregnancies, partly because of the failure in following Islamic teachings and unsafe practices but also because Muslim youth who find themselves in situations of temptation are overwhelmed. "For youth who are sheltered by their parents from any significant contact with the opposite sex, a chance encounter can result in a total loss of moral judgment," said one person. "Imagine kids who are never given the opportunity to even talk with members of the opposite sex being put in a classroom with attractive people who may show an interest in them. They just can't handle it."

Many otherwise well-meaning parents socially cripple their children by denying them the opportunity to interact with other girls and boys in an open, Islamically supervised forum. The result is that members of the opposite sex are seen as objects of fear and curiosity rather than as people —and are treated as such. "Our parents spent all of our formative years making blanket statements about the 'evils of sex," explained a 22-year old college student. "And once we get married, we're expected to conveniently forget these feelings. Many people of my age find that hard to deal with, and I think that leads to a lot of dysfunctional marriages."

THOSE WHO FALL

There are many more Muslim children than our community would like to admit who are sexually active, some unapologetically. Most, if not all, are discreet in their actions, knowing that the ensuing conflicts would be tremendous. They seem content with living dual lives, one for the mosque and one for themselves. Few, if any, reconcile their behavior with Islam, and most readily accept and believe that what they are doing is considered a major sin in Islam, seeking instead to avoid thinking or talking about the consequences. "It's amazing, really," said one observer. "People who otherwise fast and avoid alcohol will readily jump into someone's bed and not even think about it the following day. These people have moral blinders on when it comes to sex."

Most people involved treat it as a personal weakness or a failure in character, thereby avoiding responsibility for their actions. "I can't help it," said one youth. "Of the typical sex—drugs—rock and roll sampler of temptations that are available to me, the only one I can't resist is sex. Everything else is relatively easy, but that one isn't."

GOD WILL BE MORE MERCIFUL THAN MY PARENTS

For those rare occasions where a Muslim girl finds herself pregnant with an unwanted baby, the option exercised is almost always abortion, usually without consent or knowledge of the parents. The dilemma of choosing abortion in cases such as these can be devastating to those who, already racked with guilt over the consequences of their first major sin, find themselves forced to commit a second major one. "You're placed in a situation where you fear your parents more than you fear God Himself," said one young woman who found herself in this situation. "Knowingly choosing abortion was the most difficult thing I ever had to do, but at the time I was convinced that God would be more merciful than my parents."

WHAT ADVICE DO MUSLIM YOUTH HAVE FOR THEIR PEERS?

Muslim parents have little idea how knowledgeable, as well as how wise, their children are when it comes to dealing with sexual pressure. When asked to give advice to their peers, much of what they said reflected an understanding based on a great deal of personal experience and observation. "If Islam is really important to you, and you really believe that it prescribes what is best for you in the long run, then no amount of pressure should convince you," said one college-aged woman. "In a situation like that, you should take five minutes to cool down and collect your thoughts. You'll probably change your mind."

Another person explained, "Sex is an act between two people observed by God, and it should be performed in marriage with the blessing of God." Others showed a change of heart after living a sexually active lifestyle for a period of time. "I really didn't feel much moral obligation when I was younger," said one. "But now that my views and principles have changed. I think that I'm as pure inside as anyone else. I've completely distanced myself from my past life and attitude, and made a commitment to myself and God to be a more responsible person. If you do try something that you regret later, you shouldn't feel that you are a bad person. You should learn from it and move on. If you don't learn from it, then that's where you'll be making the mistake."

THE PROGNOSIS

The largest gulf of understanding still remains between the parent and the youth, especially in the area of sexuality. Sex is a natural part of life, and when questions arise, they can be discussed in a mature way without actually condoning certain behavior. Fear seems to do little in the way of preventing or curtailing certain behavior (in most cases, it can actually push kids over the edge), but in families where there is open discussion of these topics, there appears to be a stronger and more principled stand.

As in most child-parent relationships, communication is the key. In households where children obey Islam and its rules simply out of fear of the parent, the overwhelming majority either leave their Islam at home when they go out or find their thin veneer of protection easily cracked by temptation. "Your parents can't be with you forever—sooner or later you will be faced with your own decisions, and your parents won't be around to tell you what to do," one person said. The most stable youths governed their actions through God-consciousness which came through learning and education not parental pressure—and walked through the proverbial fire unharmed.

The topic occurred to me when I heard some discussions about the "equality" of man and woman in Islam and when some rejected the principle of accepting man as the head of the family. In most of these discussions many Western concepts were referred to as scientifically irrefutable, many Quranic verses were arbitrarily interpreted and many Traditions(Prophet's sayings) were ignored and described as unauthoritative. I could easily discern the motives behind such arguments and how most of them were the result of the Western social problematic structure, added to the non-Islamic ideology which prevails over the judgment of individuals in such societies.

8

A CASE AGAINST PORNOGRAPHY

SHAHID ATHAR

Question: My wife was taught that God says sex is something dirty and its only purpose is to bring children into the world. Is that what the Bible teaches? MH

Answer from Billy Graham: No. It is not. God gave sex to the human race and the Bible reminds us, "Do not call anything impure that God has made clean" (Acts 10:15). However, just like anything else God has given us, we can misuse this gift, twisting it and perverting it into something selfish and evil. But that only underlines our need to commit our sexual drive to God and ask Him to help us control it and recover His purposes for it in our own lives. God meant for the sexual relationship between husband and wife to be a physical sign of their commitment to one another, of their inner joy and oneness. That is one reason why God's purposes for sex can only be fulfilled within the commitment of marriage. (Tribune Media Services. *Indianapolis Star* August 5, 1995).

Prophet Muhammad (ﷺ) has said about usury, "A time will come when usury will reach the people like 'musk' (perfume). That is to say, "It will reach everyone whether they want it or not." In the same way, to some extent, nudity and pornography affects all of us whether we want it or not. Just turn on the TV to watch the evening news and you will be confronted with a young woman in a bikini to advertise for one-calorie Pepsi or for feminine hygiene products or for nutritious cereal. If you want some more action, you can watch the soap operas or prime time programs like "Full House" or late night movies. It reaches also in the written media, in magazines, newspapers and in music programs like MTV and Friday night video, etc.

It is not enough to say to Muslim youth that Islam prohibits such things. They ask for the reasoning process behind why it is wrong, what it leads to and so forth. They will not accept, "Don't watch it," when they ask, "Why?" and the answer comes back, "Because I said so." They ask to discuss the pros and cons to arrive at an intelligent answer. The proponents of nudity present the following argument:

1. It is protected by freedom of speech. The response is that the First Amendment is misunderstood and misapplied. Yes, we have certain rights and certain freedoms, but there is a concept of limited freedom. As long as my freedom does not affect someone else's freedom, it may be okay. If I smoke in my own closet, dance naked in my own bedroom, I am affecting only myself, but if I do the same thing outside, I am encroaching on the freedom of other people. Just like we do not like to get second-hand smoke, we do not have to accept second-hand nudity and pornography. Therefore, this is a wrong definition of freedom of expression.

2. It is harmless entertainment as compared to the violence on TV and in the movies. Response: True, in the short term, nudity and pornography appear to be less harmful than the violence shown on TV and in the movies. However, the long-term effect is much more serious and sometimes the two are tied together. It is a form of addiction. Ted Bundy, the serial killer, admitted that his criminal behavior began by watching movies on bondage and pornography. Child pornography is another disease which has contributed to 500,000 cases of incest involving father and daughter per year in this country. Child slave trade for sex involves 5 million children worldwide.

3. It is educational. Response: If at all true, it is a poor quality of edu-

cation. Most of the lessons on anatomy are given to medical students these days on a calendar or a plastic replica. It is not necessary to show live human bodies and sex ads to impart education. Even sex education, as such, is more of a theory than practice. How can a person receiving such a vivid education refrain himself from practicing on others? This is the reason for more than 100,000 rapes being committed annually in this country and the majority of date rapes are not even reported. How can bondage be called "education?" Positions of sex can be learned after marriage by experiment rather than by memorizing books or movies.

If it is not necessary to teach baby ducks how to swim, why is it necessary for teenagers to be taught the education of sexual techniques before they are expected to engage in them?

HARMFUL EFFECTS OF NUDITY AND PORNOGRAPHY

1. Degradation of women. Women and their skin are being used to advertise every product, cosmetic, dress, perfume and even medication. It is a form of oppression of women and a form of enslaving them. Many of the exercise videos are using obscene positions to sell those programs. Many of the unnatural sex acts shown in some of the x-rated moves are committed by force and under threat. Many of the tortures which are shown in bondage are against the will of women.

2. Watching nudity desensitizes men and women to normal sexual stimulus. People get used to it and therefore this is the most common cause of psychological impotency in this country. Just by becoming used to these in order to get an arousal, they have to perform some more weird acts than plain, simple nudity can provide.

3. Nudity and pornography are an addiction which leads to other crimes including drugs, murder, rape, abduction, child molestation, and incest. One leads to another until a person pays for that crime behind bars for many years to come. It is not as innocuous as people claim. It is a perversion. There are clubs of sex alcoholics just like Alcoholics Anonymous or AA where people share their previous experiences in order to enter therapy.

4. Finally, it is a waste of time. The time that is spend on vain desires and pursuit of happiness at the cost of others can be utilized in many con-

structive ways to include improving their knowledge by reading good books, doing housework, sports, exercise or perhaps of remembrance of God because to Him is our return.

Pornography, thus, is neither educational nor entertainment, but a disease and an addiction and Muslims should avoid it.

GENERAL INDEX

A

Abortion (s), 1, 5, 6, 8, 11, 21, 28, 30-31, 47, 65, 68, 70, 78
Adam, 0, 27, 51
Adams J., 19
Adultery, 12-13, 41, 49, 51, 68, 70
Afro-American, 16
AIDS, 4, 10, 17
Alcoholics Anonymous, 83
American Cancer Society, 19
American Muslim, 75
American Virgin, 11
Americans, 21, 75, 77
Arab, 16, 59, 63

B

Bible, 13, 81
Billy Graham, 81
Biological Factor, 35, 40
Bradley, 19
Brooks Cole, 58
Bukhari, 2, 14, 19

C

Christian (s), 46, 71
Chromosome, 37-39
Companions, 2, 12, 32
Concept of Adultery In Islam, 12
Concept of Marriage In Islam, 13
Creator, 16, 31, 50, 67
Cyndi Lauper, 11

D

D. B. Lynn, 58
Day of Resurrection, 31, 45
Defense Fund, 9, 19
Disease Control, 19
Divorce, 13, 15, 46-47, 55-56, 67, 73
DNA, 36
Dr. Abd, 45, 54
Dr. Abu Saud, 0, 63, 74

Dr. Mahmood Abu Saud, 63
Dr. Nelson, 9
Dracula of Hormones, 19

E

Edward Westermack, 48
Effects of Melatonins, 19
Eight National Evangelical Churchs, 19
El Tigani Adam Hammad, 27
Elam, 19
Endocrinology, 19
European, 16
Eve, 51
Evolution, 36-37, 45, 50-51

F

Family Life Services, 59
Farhad Khan, 75
Father Bruce, 10
Father James Burtchaell, 21
Freudian, 28

G

Gender Interaction, 25
Gender Relations Attitude Survey, 59, 61
Gender Relations Attitude Survey of Muslim Youth, 59
God-consciousness, 79
Godfearing, 14

H

Hadith, 19, 58, 67
Hakim, 14
Hammudah Abd, 58
Harmful Effects of Nudity, 83
Havelock Ellis, 47
Hazards of Early Sex, 9
Hindu, 71
Homosexuality, 28, 35, 43, 47
Hormones, 19, 38-40, 43
Human Biology, 37, 42

I

Ibn Massoud, 14
Imam Abduh, 53-54

Indo-Pakistani, 59, 63
Islamic Concept Of Sexuality, 12
Islamic Horizon, 66
Islamic Law, 54, 56
Islamic School, 16-17, 60
Islamic Sex Education, 16, 61
Islamic Shariah, 46
Islamic Society of Toledo, 63
Islamic Sunday, 2, 17, 60

J

Jews, 56, 71
John Hopkins, 9
Judaism, 46
Judas Priest, 11
Justinian, 46

L

Ladies Home Journal, 19
Law Maker, 64
London, 34

M

M. A. Diamond, 58
Madonna, 11
Mahmoud Abu Saud, 35
Marion Wright Elderman, 9
Marriage of Muslim, 14-15
Marriage of Muslim Girls, 15
Masturbation, 32, 67-68
Medical Aspects of Human, 19
Medical Aspects of Human Sexuality, 19
Melvin Anchell, 27
Misunderstood Religion, 29, 34
Modesty, 2, 13, 17, 73
Motherhood, 42, 52, 55
MTV, 10, 82
Muhammad Abduh, 54
Muhammad Qutb, 29, 34
Muslim Organizations, 14
Muslim Physician, 27, 29-31, 33
Muslim Youth, 0, 14, 59, 63, 65, 67, 69, 71, 73-75, 77-78, 82

SIDNEY B. COULTER LIBRARY
Onondaga Community College
Syracuse, New York 13215